HARRY STYLES

THE UNAUTHORIZED BIOGRAPHY

HARRY STYLES

THE UNAUTHORIZED BIOGRAPHY

ALICE MONTGOMERY

MICHAEL JOSEPH
an imprint of
PENGUIN BOOKS

MICHAEL JOSEPH

Published by the Penguin Group
Penguin Books Ltd, 80 Strand, London WC2R 0RL, England
Penguin Group (USA) Inc., 375 Hudson Street, New York, New York 10014, USA
Penguin Group (Canada), 90 Eglinton Avenue East, Suite 700, Toronto, Ontario, Canada M4P 2Y3
(a division of Pearson Penguin Canada Inc.)
Penguin Ireland, 25 St Stephen's Green, Dublin 2, Ireland (a division of Penguin Books Ltd)
Penguin Group (Australia), 707 Collins Street, Melbourne, Victoria 3008, Australia
(a division of Pearson Australia Group Pty Ltd)
Penguin Books India Pvt Ltd, 11 Community Centre,
Panchsheel Park, New Delhi – 110 017, India
Penguin Group (NZ), 67 Apollo Drive, Rosedale, Auckland 0632, New Zealand
(a division of Pearson New Zealand Ltd)
Penguin Books (South Africa) (Pty) Ltd, Block D, Rosebank Office Park, 181 Jan Smuts Avenue,
Parktown North, Gauteng 2193, South Africa

Penguin Books Ltd, Registered Offices: 80 Strand, London WC2R 0RL, England

www.penguin.com

First published 2013
001

Copyright © Alice Montgomery, 2013

The moral right of the author has been asserted

Set in 13/16pt Minion Pro
Typeset by Jouve (UK), Milton Keynes
Printed in Great Britain by Clays Ltd, St Ives plc

A CIP catalogue record for this book is available from the British Library

ISBN: 978–0–718–17843–7

www.greenpenguin.co.uk

ALWAYS LEARNING   PEARSON

Contents

1

When Harry Met Caroline

t was 2011, a full year since the series of *The X Factor* that had made superstars out of the teen sensation One Direction, and its sister programme, *The Xtra Factor*, had a new presenter. She was Caroline Flack, an attractive thirty-two-year-old brunette, who had made her name hosting a series of reality television programmes since 2002. Lively and vivacious, she was popular with the viewers – especially the male ones. She had had her pick of men to date, but the next one she chose was going to raise eyebrows and attract far more attention than either of the people involved could possibly have foreseen.

Even before the couple got together, there were hints of what was to come. One Direction was the hottest group on the planet, and its hottest member was seventeen-year-old Harry Styles. With his big eyes, youthful appearance and trademark mop of wildly unruly hair, he was turning into a major heart-throb, massively popular with the female fans, and with a cheeky grin that was proving irresistible to an awful lot of girls across the world. Naturally, there was a huge amount of interest in what kind of girl would appeal to him, and Harry was only too happy to make it clear. Frankie Sandford from The Saturdays would do for him, it seemed. 'I've been in love with Frankie ever since I was about eight and she was in S Club Juniors,' he told the *Daily Star Sunday*. 'I even had posters of her. I'd love to kiss her. Frankie and Caroline Flack are my favourites. They are both hot.'

Unlike most young male fans, though, Harry was in a position to do something about his crushes. Since appearing on *The X Factor* a year earlier, the One Direction boys had been travelling the world, moving in show-business circles, and they now had a major hit on their hands with their number-one single 'What Makes You Beautiful'. He followed up the interview with a comment on *The X Factor* website: 'If Caroline Flack is reading this, say "Hi" from me. She is gorgeous!' There were reports that he was even trying to persuade Tim Dean, a producer on *The Xtra Factor*, to send Caroline a tweet persuading her to date him. Even so, no one could have forecast that Harry and Caroline were shortly to become one of show business's most unlikely couples.

Indeed, initially it seemed that if Caroline was going to pair off with anyone, it would be her *Xtra* co-host, Olly Murs. Olly gave a deliberately provocative interview, hinting that something might happen between them: 'We do some great flirting,' he told the *Sun*. 'I get to work with *The X Factor*, which is the best show on TV, and I get to work with someone gorgeous like Caroline. Happy days. We get to have a laugh and cuddle all day and we have a kiss here and there. We get on well and it's great to have that chemistry both on camera and off.' Not that anything had actually happened, of course, other than the fact that the two of them had established themselves as an excellent presenting duo, with plenty of chemistry between them.

'Sometimes relationships build over time, and at the moment we're concentrating on the job in hand, but we do have a good flirt,' he continued. 'She's attractive and we have a laugh, so when the show finishes in December, who knows what will happen?' What would happen, of course, was that Caroline would be splashed all over the front pages with her much younger boyfriend, but what Olly and Caroline both knew, and Harry had spent the last year finding out, is that all publicity is good publicity, and a hint of romance between two high-profile celebrities won't do either of them any harm. It also made the point that Caroline was a very attractive woman, something young men were already aware of. The will they/won't they question delighted viewers, as both Caroline and Olly realized, although both also admitted that they were single. Not, in Caroline's case, for long though.

The occasion was an *X Factor* aftershow party towards the end of October 2011, at the W Hotel in London. Caroline and Harry were both present and, according to fellow partygoers, it didn't take long for Harry to make a move. He headed straight for her, engaged her in conversation, and then, much to the bemusement of everyone else present, moved in for a kiss. More than that, the seventeen-year old and the thirty-two-year old were then seen leaving the party together and sharing a cab, although nothing more happened that night and the two went their separate ways. Harry took to Twitter: 'Sometimes things happen and you suddenly get a whole new outlook on life,' he tweeted, as well he might.

At first, this exceedingly unlikely pairing was met with a certain degree of hilarity. It was just so unlikely – the fifteen-year age gap might not have loomed so large had they both been in their twenties and thirties, but Harry was still a teenager. No one could believe it would last a week, let alone three months. There was increased hilarity when observers noted two further tweets: Caroline's: 'Woke up with the sorest throat and huge glands!!!' Followed a few hours later by Harry's: 'Woke up with man flu and a sore throat today.' It didn't take too much to work out what was going on there.

As it happened, Harry had already proved himself to be something of a ladies' man. While sharing a flat with fellow band mate Louis Tomlinson, Harry had brought so many girls back to the flat that Louis, who was in a relationship with model Eleanor Calder, complained that the neighbours might think they were running a nail bar. 'The worst thing about living with Harry is the constant stream of women he is getting through our door,' he said. 'It's relentless.' But that constant stream was about to be replaced by just the one.

Following an appearance with Lady Gaga on *The X Factor*, One Direction's schedule was busier than ever, and yet still the unlikely romance continued to develop behind the scenes. Harry couldn't help but drop the odd hint in public, too. 'I'd love to take Caroline out,' he quipped. 'How about McDonald's? But I wouldn't want to share her with Olly.'

In reality, he knew perfectly well that Caroline and Olly weren't dating. Harry had learned a great deal over the last year, including the fact that in the world of showbiz, things are not always as they seem. His other band mates hinted that something was up: 'Harry's found the one now,' said Louis, although he refused to go into detail about who it was. One Direction then appeared on *The Xtra Factor*, where Harry was asked which contestant in the current series he fancied. 'They're all a bit young for me,' he replied.

And it seemed that Caroline wasn't the only woman to have noticed the young pop star: Peaches Geldof, at twenty-two also an older woman, was so taken with Harry she asked for his phone number. Harry duly obliged, but later ruefully admitted he'd handed over the wrong number. 'She must hate me,' he said in a revealing interview with *OK!* magazine. 'If she's reading this, say hello next time you see me. I might give you the right number.' In that same interview he also made it clear that while he was only seventeen, he was certainly no innocent. Harry had already made love, and the first time he did so, he was scared he'd made the girl pregnant, although they'd used condoms and so should have been 'safe'. In the event, everything was fine, he added. On another occasion he told a female admirer he was gay in order to discourage her. Since he was obviously already an experienced seducer, at least deflowering Harry wasn't going to appear on the list of charges that would shortly be laid at Caroline's door.

It wasn't long after that that it became clear the two really were an item. They were seen eating out together, and it certainly wasn't at McDonald's; rather they were spotted at the very chi-chi Asia de Cuba restaurant in London's smart St Martin's Lane Hotel, a venue favoured by many a famous star. Caroline was seen in the lobby waiting for her beau, after which the pair dined with another couple. They only had eyes for each other, and were not only flirting openly, but left together and in a chauffeured car that drove them off into the night.

They were, however, rather shaken at the almost immediate backlash from One Direction fans, who took to social media sites to vent their spleen. Many of the fans seemed to think that if they couldn't have Harry, then no one else should have him either, and certainly not someone old enough to be his much older big sister. Really unpleasant comments, such as, 'If Caroline Flack flirts with my boyfriend [Harry] I will personally hunt her down and shoot her,' appeared online, together with, 'I want to kill you, Caroline Flack. Harry is mine, bitch,' and she 'should be having kids not dating them'. This prompted Caroline to take to Twitter herself. 'I'm close friends with Harry,' she tweeted. 'He's one of the nicest people I know. I don't deserve death threats.' Some tweeters supported her: 'I don't even care any more,' tweeted one. 'If Harry wants to date an oldie, let him be.' Another told the fans to grow up, while another expressed disbelief that there should be actual death threats.

Meanwhile Olly, who hadn't exactly lost his *Xtra Factor* playmate, but who could no longer hint that they were on the verge of becoming a couple, started making alarming statements of his own. 'If I had to kiss a man, it would be Justin Timberlake,' he declared. 'He's an idol of mine. I like Michael Bublé, too. I was star-struck when I met him.' What the two men thought of this is unknown, but there was a lot of joking that now Caroline had run off with Harry, Olly had decided he was gay.

In fact, Olly wasn't the only man to have had his nose put out of joint by the new relationship: Caroline's ex, the rock star Dave Danger, was also far from thrilled by the news. The couple had broken up in 2009, but Dave, former drummer with indie rock band The Holloways, had been hoping for a reconciliation. At first, like everyone else, he dismissed the rumours that Caroline and Harry were an item because it just seemed too unlikely, but eventually he was forced to confront the truth.

'They only split because their work schedules meant they hardly saw each other,' a friend of Dave's told the *Daily Star*. 'But there was no doubt that they were still in love with each other. Caroline was very open with the fact she had hoped for a reconciliation. Over the last few weeks, they've been spending more and more time together, but suddenly she completely cooled off and has left Dave hanging. It's come at the same time as she was linked with Harry. At first Dave just laughed and thought the rumours about her kissing him were a practical joke. Harry is just a kid. But as Caroline started to dodge dates and fail to return texts, he thinks she must be serious about this kid. He thinks she's lost the plot.

He wants to talk to her about her actions but she cut him dead.'

Indeed, unlikely as it seemed, the pair were giving the impression that they were serious, and there were reports that Caroline had asked Harry to move in with her. Harry played it down in public, but Olly gave the game away when he said that Harry had a penchant for older women: 'He's always openly spoken to me about how much he likes Caroline,' he said.

In many ways, the situation was highly unusual, and not just because of the age gap. Usually, boy band members are discouraged from having girlfriends, or are at least told to be discreet about them, on the grounds that their presence could discourage their female fans. In the case of One Direction, however, no one was trying to hide anything. Harry's remark about Caroline – 'We're good mates and we hang out a lot; we just get on really well so we're friends – we'll see what happens' – fooled no one. In fact, the boys were positively encouraged to go out with girls: Zayn Malik had had a relationship with fellow *X Factor* contestant Rebecca Ferguson, and the boys made no bones about their appreciation of the women they met. In many ways it was a healthier situation than that experience by many boy bands before them: in Take That's first incarnation, before they split, the boys were encouraged to promote a squeaky-clean image, which wasn't the reality at all. Years later, stories about groupies hiding in cupboards came out, but at the time the pressure of having to conform was one of the stresses that drove Robbie

Williams to a near breakdown and led to him leaving the group. No one wanted to take any chances with something similar happening to One Direction. The boys were young men having the time of their lives, and no one wanted to stop them from enjoying every moment.

While Harry was being coy about his new relationship, however, Caroline was less so. They were an item and had been for a while now, and she was still getting a lot of stick about the age gap. 'I feel like I shouldn't have to worry about what I do, but it's a social thing that people aren't accepting of big age gaps,' she said in an interview with *Now* magazine. 'I keep thinking, What have I done wrong? But I haven't done anything wrong. What's hard for me to get my head around is people saying it's disgusting. I don't think it is. Some people tend to see the negative immediately and that's what I find strange. If two people like each other and get on, why does anyone else find a negative in it? I know it's human nature for everyone to gossip. But why say it's bad? No one's being hurt.' And of the death threats on Twitter, she added, 'It went too far. It's a form of bullying from people who are hiding behind a computer. I knew they were just a minority of One Direction fans and all very young – it's a kind of fanatical obsession. I can't take it seriously or I'd never come out of my house. He [Harry] told me, "Don't listen to Twitter." So he became the mature one at that point!'

Harry was pictured arriving at Caroline's house in the evening and departing, looking exhausted, the following morning – by now the attention surrounding him was starting to set him apart from the rest of the gang. Comedian David Walliams was one of the first to comment on that. 'I am not the key audience as I am not a ten-year-old girl, but I am a fan of the band and I like Harry,' he told the *Daily Star*. 'I bet Harry infuriates the rest of One Direction.' If he did, they were smart enough to shut up about it, but it was true that he stood out from the rest. All of the boys generated huge amounts of attention wherever they went, but Harry provoked a particular hysteria, and his choice of girlfriend only made him *more* of an object of devotion, not *less*. If nothing else, it certainly proved that Harry wasn't attracted to vacuous airheads.

Still Caroline continued to get a lot of stick: 'We have fun. What's wrong with that?' she protested in a TV interview, but the fans carried on complaining. Harry was more opaque: 'People should think more before they tweet stuff,' he observed. 'Never complain, never explain.' Even Olly tried to get angry tweeters to back off: 'Harry is a good-looking lad and most girls in this country would want to snog him,' he said. 'Nothing's concrete. It's all good. Everyone tweets what they want but no one knows the inside truth – that's private. All this taking pictures and stuff is unfair.' The last reference may have been a reference to the fact that Caroline had been pictured doing the walk of shame from Harry's flat early one morning.

Other doubters, who said the relationship was a 'showmance', purely for the publicity it engendered, were clearly wrong. By now a debate about the appropriateness or otherwise of the relationship was being played out in the national press, along-side real-life stories about 'cougars' (women who date much younger men).

Briefly, it looked as if the relationship might be turning serious. One Direction was setting off on a twenty-four-date tour of the UK and Ireland in December, and Caroline was seen looking stricken after seeing Harry off, having given him a lift to Watford in Hertfordshire. Harry, it must be said, didn't look quite so devastated, not least because the tour was being considered a measure of the boys' popularity, and so far it was working out spectacularly well: the dates were all sold out and the band had received an ecstatic reception at every venue. The career side of Harry's life was certainly going according to plan.

Early in the new year, Caroline took time off to go on holi-day to India, while Harry and the boys continued on their highly successful tour, but once back in the country, she defied her critics by turning up to a One Direction gig. For this, she was rewarded with the sight of banners bearing the message, 'Flack off, Caroline.' There was also a stallholder selling whistles, who told concert-goers to 'whistle if you hate Caroline Flack'. All 150 whistles sold out. Caroline largely ignored it, but she wouldn't have been human if she hadn't minded a little. She was coming under fire from all sides – not just from One Direction fans but from any number of the self-appointed guardians of public morality who loudly con-demned her every move. Even Rebecca Ferguson, now aged twenty-five, who had dated nineteen-year-old Zayn, got in on the act: 'I think there's something not right about Caroline and Harry's relationship,' she said. 'For me and Zayn it was different, because he was eighteen, so at least we could go for a drink in a bar together, and he was old enough to make his own decisions. But Harry is too young for that . . . there is so much more of an age gap.'

In some ways, of course, she was right: Harry was still very young. Reports that the couple were moving in together proved wide of the mark, though, and although they continued to see a great deal of each other, the strain began to show. No one would have enjoyed the public abuse Caroline was subjected to, and even if Harry had had a girlfriend who was the same age as him, seventeen is still extremely young to get serious about anybody. On top of that, One Direction clearly had a massive future ahead of them. Did he really want to commit himself to someone when this huge opportunity was opening up in his life?

To add to the pressure, One Direction were on the verge of attempting to break into the US market, which is an extremely difficult feat for any British artist: many have tried but remarkably few have succeeded. However, the momentum had built up behind them in the UK to such an extent that it was clearly the right time for One Direction to give it a push and have a go. Consequently, they were about to spend the next two months touring the States. Their mentor Simon Cowell was one of the few Brits who had built up a presence in the US, and he would be able to guide them in a venture that could change their lives even further.

So it was that, towards the end of January 2012, the relationship that had provoked such controversy and comment gradually wound down. It seemed that Caroline had taken it a little more seriously than Harry, and was said to be rather downhearted about the whole thing, while Harry had realized the pair had no further to go. There were also rumours of concerns that the relationship was damaging One Direction's clean-cut image, although given the fact that this wasn't Harry's last relationship with an older woman, that seems unlikely. Whatever the case, it was all over.

'Harry is being realistic about the whole thing,' a friend told the *Daily Mirror*. 'He's going off to America in a couple of days and he wants to be able to commit fully to making the band a success in the States. They'll be back for The Brits, but all in all they'll be away for two months. It's a long time to be apart, especially with so much going on. Harry's young. He's just not ready for a long-distance relationship. He really likes Caroline and he doesn't want to hurt her, but he doesn't want to be tied down.' Harry took to Twitter to announce that it had been a mutual decision. 'Please know I didn't "dump" Caroline. This was a mutual decision,' he tweeted. 'She is one of the kindest, sweetest people I know. Please respect that.'

The fans were mightily relieved, and so was someone a lot closer to home: Harry's father, Des. Like a great many people, Des felt pretty jaundiced about the whole thing. It was 'ridiculous', he said, adding, 'thirty-two or whatever she was and Harry, seventeen, that's a bit extreme.'

The one person who was relaxed about it was Harry's

mother, Anne Cox, to whom he was extremely close. She and Caroline had got on very well, by all accounts, and she took a pragmatic view. 'I've never really thought whether it would be a problem. Personality is more important than anything else,' she told the *Mirror*. 'I think the younger you are the more people will make of an age gap. If Harry was twenty years older there wouldn't be an issue. My husband was ten years older than me and it didn't bother me one way or the other.'

Caroline put a brave face on it, turning up at the National Television Awards with newly darkened brunette hair, and whatever private sadness she might have felt at the end of the relationship, at least she would no longer be subjected to endless criticism from One Direction fans – and just about everyone else. Their relationship could never really have had a future – apart from the age gap, Harry was on the verge of a whole new life. He would also prove that those reports that he was a ladies' man were spot on as, over the coming months, he was linked to several women, a fair few of whom were considerably older than him. Harry clearly had a type.

That was not, however, quite the end of it. Over a year after Harry and Caroline split up, and after Harry had been linked to a string of other women, he was still in touch with her, sending her saucy text messages. 'Caroline jokes: "Dirty Harry's at it again,"' a friend of the television presenter told *Now* magazine. 'He's been sending her texts full of innuendoes. One said: "You're looking hot." She knows he's a smooth operator, but she likes the compliments and admits she still fancies the pants off him.' Nevertheless, the two of them had moved on.

It was the end of an extraordinary episode, which had attracted huge amounts of attention, and from which Harry had emerged with his dignity and maturity pretty much intact. Harry's whole life had taken an extraordinary turn ever since he had appeared on *The X Factor* a year earlier, going overnight from schoolboy to heart-throb. And this was only the beginning of a sensational ride. So just who is Harry Styles? How had One Direction come into being? And how on earth did he become the massive star he is today?

2

First Steps

Nicole Scherzinger was feeling thoughtful. *The X Factor* guest judge and former Pussycat Doll had been impressed by five young men who had appeared on the seventh series of the show, but although they'd made it through to the auditions and boot-camp, for some reason they'd been unable to get through to the 'Boys' category at the judges' house stage of the show. One boy in particular stood out during the auditions: a sixteen-year-old called Harry Styles, who had impressed the judges with his rendition of Stevie Wonder's 'Isn't She Lovely'. Nicole in particular had told him his voice was 'lovely'. Her fellow judge and *X Factor* supremo Simon Cowell agreed to a certain extent, voting Harry through, but telling him he was going to need some voice coaching. There was clearly some talent there, but how to harness it best?

The same applied to four other young men, who had all made individual appearances on the show: Niall Horan, Liam Payne (who had appeared on *The X Factor* in 2008 when he was only fourteen – Cowell had told him then to go away and come back in two years' time), Zayn Malik and Louis Tomlinson. Regular judges Dannii Minogue and Cheryl Cole were absent – Dannii was on maternity leave while Cheryl was suffering from malaria – so Nicole was there as a guest judge. For the same reason, the show's producers decided to axe the live audience participation element, and so judges Simon and Louis Walsh split the participating acts into their four categories: Boys, Girls, Over 25s (later changed to Over 28s) and Groups. This time the boys didn't do so well, and none of them made it through on their own merits. However, Nicole had an idea, which Simon also claims credit for: why not put the five of them together and let them go through into the Groups category? It might just work.

For the boys, *The X Factor* seemed at first to be an absolute disaster. Harry was turned down flat: 'I think you're so young,' said Louis Walsh in a judgement that would later come back to bite him. 'I don't think you have enough experience or confidence yet; I'm going to say no.' Harry was duly sent off and later confessed to the *Daily Mirror*, 'I was gutted not to make it.'

Cheryl was similarly crushing to Niall. Zayn and Louis were also doing badly, and although Liam initially prompted Simon to say that his rendition of 'Cry Me A River' was 'absolutely incredible' – 'Whatever "it" is, you've got it,' added Cheryl – he too performed badly at the bootcamp stage. All the boys were disheartened, with Zayn echoing Harry's sentiments when he said, 'I felt crushed.'

'I phoned my parents and told them,' added Liam. 'My parents are always helping me with everything and they believed in me so much. I felt I'd failed and let them down.'

But all was not lost. Nicole wasn't the only one who had an inkling that together they would be greater than the sum of their parts; that seasoned industry observer Simon Cowell thought so, too. 'They were solo artists to begin with,' he told *Rolling Stone* magazine some time later, when the newly formed band had turned into the hottest item on the planet. 'Each of them individually had very good auditions. We had high hopes for two or three of them in particular, and then it all kind of fell apart at one of the latter stages. Interestingly, when they left, I had a bad feeling that maybe we shouldn't have lost them and maybe there was something else we should do with them. And this is when the idea came about that we should see if they could work as a group. We invited these five guys back. They were the only five we cared about.'

The boys certainly seemed to have something in common. All were from the north of England, with the exception of Niall, who is Irish; all were in their mid-to-late teens, and three had had previous musical experience. More to the point, all five of them had exactly the qualities that appeal to young female fans: they were fresh-faced, not too overtly threatening in a masculine sense and all, as teen idols must, had very, very good hair. Right from the start, Harry stood out – especially with regards to his hair. Besides, boy bands always go down better with very young female fans, as opposed to solo artists, who tend to appeal to a slightly older audience, which might have something to do with getting five for the price of one.

The boys were summoned to see Nicole, who spelt out the

new game plan. Four of them quite literally jumped for joy, but Liam, who felt cautious due to his previous *X Factor* experience, asked for time to think about it – 'I had to decide whether I was ready to throw all that work away,' he later explained. 'I'd been trying so hard to do the solo thing, but saying "no" would have meant going home with nothing.' And so he said yes.

All in all, it was quite a turn-up for the books, and not a development that anyone had expected when the seventh series of *The X Factor*, which would turn Harry and his cohorts into superstars, had started its run on 21 August 2010. In fact, of course, the series, which was presented by Dermot O'Leary on ITV1, with spin-off *The Xtra Factor* being hosted by Konnie Huq on ITV2, had spun into production some months earlier, with initial auditions taking place in June and July. Simon Cowell, Louis Walsh and Cheryl Cole were once again judges. Dannii was due to return from maternity leave in time for the judges' house stage, before which a succession of guest judges would stand in for her. Cheryl missed the Manchester auditions because of her malaria. The series was the first to be filmed in high-definition, and was constantly mired in controversy, not least because two bands were formed out of less successful solo singers, and pitch-correction software was used on the broadcast of the contestants' auditions. That said, the final was watched by over seventeen million people – the highest viewing figures in the year 2010.

The format of the show went as follows. In December 2009,

potential contestants were invited to audition. The auditions began in earnest the following June, in Glasgow, Birmingham, London, Dublin, Cardiff and Manchester. The guest judges covering for Dannii were Geri Halliwell in Glasgow, Natalie Imbruglia in Birmingham, Katy Perry in Dublin, Pixie Lott in Cardiff and Nicole Scherzinger in Manchester. There was no guest judge in London. After the auditions came bootcamp, still without Cheryl and Dannii and thus not broadcast to a live audience. This included splitting up the acts into four categories, and saw the formation of the two groups, as well as the return of Nicole as a guest judge. There then followed the judges' houses, live shows and the final.

It was in the early stages of the show that, quite unexpectedly, two acts were created out of soloists, and it consequently became clear that this series was going to attract a huge amount of attention. The boys themselves were a little uncertain about the abrupt change of plan. After all, they had each entered wanting to be a solo artist, and being turned into a manufactured boy band, albeit it by Simon Cowell and Louis Walsh, two of the most experienced men in the music industry, was a bit of a shock. Apart from anything else, would they get on?

'My first thought was, are we going to make this work when we don't know each other? It was such a leap of faith,' Liam told *WalesOnline*. 'I didn't think I would ever want to be in a group. But when I was there and it was happening, and I knew the lads a bit, there was no way I was going to say no,' Zayn chipped in.

In any case, they didn't have much choice. It was work together or leave the competition – and none of them wanted to do that. It was a case of learning fast in front of an audience of millions, as well as acquiring new musical techniques. None of them had experience of singing in harmony and, according to Zayn, they simply sang in unison for a couple of weeks until finally it all began to mesh. Most manufactured boy bands have time to rehearse in private and perfect their act before taking it to the public, to say nothing of doing as Take That did: building up a following while gaining experience and learning their trade by touring small-scale venues. None of those options was open to One Direction: they not only had to get up to speed extremely quickly, they had to do so under the critical gaze of the public. Nevertheless, they realized that this was a big opportunity, even if it wasn't the one they'd expected, so they all decided to give it a go.

To get to know one another, the boys assembled at a bungalow owned by Harry's stepfather in Cheshire. There they started on the basics, such as getting to know one another's names. They next problem centred on what they were going to be called. A boy band needs a name, and they hadn't had much time to think about one. It was actually Harry who came up with the idea of calling themselves One Direction, partly because all five of them were now moving in one direction together and partly because the one direction they were moving in was to the top of show-business success. As we'll find out later, the choice of name would prove a little controversial, as it was also the name of an American band –

which eventually led to legal action – but there was no doubting the fact that it suited the boys from the start. And it stuck. 'While we were there [in the cottage], Harry came up with the name One Direction,' Zayn explained. 'Another name we thought of was USP, and Liam's dad came up with Status Single – which was just awful.'

The bootcamp stage of the competition, which the boys had now got through to as a group, was held at London's Wembley Arena. It started on 22 July, and was due to be broadcast on 25 and 26 September. This was when the 211 contestants were divided into four categories and the competition started to get serious. After receiving vocal training, each category performed one song: the Boys sang 'Man In The Mirror'; the Girls sang 'If I Were A Boy'; the Over 25s sang 'Poker Face' and the Groups sang 'Nothing's Gonna Stop Us Now'. At the end of the first day, the number of acts was cut from 211 to 108, and on the second day, creative director Brian Friedman came on to give a dance lesson, although no judging was done on that particular performance. The competition was well and truly underway.

Nicole returned as a guest judge while the various performers were called upon to show their mettle. They were given a list of forty songs and each act had to choose one to perform. This was when, at Nicole's suggestion, the categories were changed slightly so that the Over-25s became Over-28s, the Boys and Girls categories changed to encompass singers aged sixteen to twenty-eight rather than twenty-five, something everyone was relieved about as some of the stronger contestants came from the upper age range. Because of the range of talent, some other changes were made to the format, too: usually six acts from each category progressed to the judges' house stage of the show, but this year that would be increased to eight.

By this stage of the proceedings, the judges started to take a personal interest in what was going on on stage. They would now be assigned various acts, in effect putting the judges in competition with each other, as well as being in a position to judge the competition on stage. Cowell was given the Groups to mentor, while Walsh had the Over-28s, and Dannii and Cheryl, who were both shortly to return, were given Boys and Girls respectively.

As it happened, One Direction wasn't the only group to be put together out of the blue in that particular series of *The X Factor*: the same thing happened to a group of solo female artists, who became the group Belle Amie. Given One Direction's subsequent success, it's often forgotten that the move was a controversial one at the time. The other groups who had entered *The X Factor* had their noses severely put out of joint, especially when the new groups began attracting a lot more attention than the ones who'd originally been on the scene. There was a lot of muttering behind the scenes that it was unfair and Cowell shouldn't have done it. Some elements of the media also started getting in on the act: rules were changing left, right and centre this year, they complained. The categories were changing, numbers going through were changing and the acts themselves were turning from one thing into another, namely solo singers into groups. Simon, who was mentoring the bands, gave his critics short shrift, pointing out that some of the most successful bands in the world had been put together by an outsider.

'To be honest the groups who turned up weren't good enough,' he told the *Daily Star* somewhat bluntly. 'And anyway, The Wanted didn't suddenly walk into each other on a High Street. The same for the Spice Girls, Westlife, Jackson Five – someone's got to be a catalyst. The groups are tough, sure, but you know what, this is where you show what you have got. I thought it was fairer to put these singers in a group rather than let them go because they weren't quite there.'

In any case, they were starting to do quite well. No band had ever won *The X Factor* before, but the boys were throwing themselves into the competition wholeheartedly, and had now got through to the next stage in the competition, the judges' house, which also saw the return of Dannii and Cheryl, who had recovered from her bout of malaria and was now restored to good health. As mentioned, eight acts were allowed through in each category, and this was where the judges became even more closely involved, taking the performers under their wing, guiding and helping them, hopefully, to win. Each judge was supported by a guest judge: Cowell by Sinitta in Marbella, Spain; Louis by Sharon Osbourne in Adare, County Limerick, Ireland; Cheryl by Will.i.am in Coworth Park, Ascot, Berkshire; and Dannii by Natalie Imbruglia in Melbourne, Australia.

All the contestants spent a week at the judges' houses and performed two songs: the judges had to eliminate five acts, leaving twelve remaining; the relevant show went out on 2 and 3 October 2010. The stakes were getting increasingly high, and it was now that very distinct personalities began to emerge, many of whom would make a name for themselves, even though they would be discarded during the process. There was Cher Lloyd, who seemed to model herself almost entirely on her mentor Cheryl Cole – there was certainly a striking resemblance between the two, alongside some concern that Cher appeared to eat hardly anything. And Katie Waissel, who became something of a hate figure on the show, appearing at times both manipulative and too outspoken. Both of them have built a career on their *X Factor* appearance, even though they didn't go on to win.

Student and single mother Rebecca Ferguson, and Matt Cardle, a painter and decorator from Little Maplestead, Essex, both stood out from the start, while another participant was the Irish singer-songwriter Mary Byrne, who was a surprise hit with the viewers. Aged fifty-one, Mary was considerably older than some of the other contestants; having given up a promising singing career in her twenties, she was working at Tesco before she appeared on the show. *The X Factor* thrust her to prominence with a successful performing career, giving her the chance to fulfil the ambitions she'd had decades earlier.

On top of that, some of the acts who hadn't made it through the previous round were brought back as wildcards on the first live show on 9 October: they were Paije Richardson, Treyc Cohen, Wagner and Diva Fever. It was another move that created controversy and attracted attention: Wagner Fiuza-Carrilho, fifty-four, was another slightly older contestant, an over-the-top Brazilian with a strong personality and a knack for attracting attention. Treyc Cohen, meanwhile, had been in the sixth series of *The X Factor* – confusingly, in series six she was in the Over-Twenty-fives category, but because of the change in age range, in series seven she was with the Girls – and was the cause of a fair few raised eyebrows when it emerged that she'd actually won a recording contract before she appeared on the seventh series of the show, something that's meant to be strictly forbidden. It was said that *The X Factor* had been trying to release Treyc from her management contract, and it subsequently emerged that Katie Waissel had also had to be removed from a contract in the United States after her audition.

This year's *X Factor* was full of strong, extremely competitive personalities, all of whom were desperate to win. And Cowell, who knew full well that all the bitchiness, backstabbing, rumour, gossip, malice and controversy would only increase the show's ratings – as indeed they did – was delighted at the diversity of his line-up. 'If people are badly behaved sometimes – so what? I'm fine with that, at least they are having fun,' he said in a typically robust interview with the *Daily Star*. 'You have got to have some sort of control, but at the end of the day you want to have the personalities through so it is fun. They are entering the music business for all the right reasons. And that is not to sit in the library till three in the morning. I banned the word journey because that was a key part of it all. We got too much of this "I'm doing it for my mum who broke her ankle" nonsense. I never bought a David Bowie album when I was seventeen because Bowie was talking on *Top of the Pops* about going on a journey. You like the music and you like the lifestyle. What we are trying to avoid is seventeen-year-olds coming up with pathetic sob stories and singing songs that are too old for them in the hope they are going to be popular. I don't want this to be a popularity competition. I think it is important that it remains a talent competition. I am just trying to encourage them this year to be their age and do what they would like to do if they had a career as a pop star and for everyone to be more relaxed about it.'

It was while they were out in Marbella at Simon's house that the entrepreneur first began to realize just what he had on his hands with One Direction. The band was going to perform 'Torn' for him when, yet again, disaster struck: Louis was stung by a sea urchin and had to be rushed to hospital. Still in some considerable pain he made it back just in time: 'I limped over to where they were singing and Simon was laughing at me,' he later told the *Daily Mirror*. 'It was a nightmare but I battled through the pain.'

He was very glad he did, too. 'They're cool, they're relevant,' a clearly pleased Simon told Sinitta. 'Guys, I've gone with my heart. You're through.' Another battle had been overcome.

This series was certainly turning out to be a humdinger. The public weren't always in agreement with the judges, though, and they weren't afraid to show it: there was wide-spread fury when Cheryl sent Cher and Katie through to the finals, dropping Gamu Nhengu, who was a favourite with the viewers. Matters quickly turned nasty with the start of a Facebook campaign, condemning Cheryl for the decision, and there were reports that she had organized additional security at her home in Surrey. There were further reports that *The X Factor* itself had stepped up security as viewers became more and more emotionally involved in the outcome – no one wanted to take any risks. Still the viewing figures soared, and while Simon might have voiced contempt for anyone who saw their participation as a 'journey', the audience took a different view. There was a whole range of life stories being played out and feelings often ran high.

The live shows took place at The Fountain Studios in Wembley in north-west London, with the actual performances taking place on Saturday nights and the results being announced on Sundays. Each week had a different song theme, and the contestants were gradually whittled down by a process of elimination.

One Direction's first song as a group, during the judge's house stage, was an acoustic version of 'Torn', which was commonly considered to be an excellent performance and a vindication of everyone who thought they would work well together as a group. In week one of the live shows they sang 'Viva La Vida'; in week two the theme was Musical Heroes and they sang 'My Life Would Suck Without You'. Everyone was really beginning to take notice: Cheryl called them 'cute', Dannii called them 'five heart-throbs' (she was certainly right there) and Simon told them they were the most exciting band in the country right now. It was heady stuff.

They were doing well with the public, too, getting through week after week after week. Their next performance was 'Nobody Knows', followed by 'Total Eclipse Of The Heart', and when Belle Amie were eliminated in week four of the competition, they were left as Simon's only remaining act. Of course, as far as Cowell was concerned, whoever won would benefit him as they would sign up to the Syco record label, but in terms of creating an exciting dynamic between the panel of judges, it was extremely successful. Not that there seemed much danger of One Direction being eliminated. They were never once in the bottom two – the danger zone where someone has to leave – and seemed to improve with each show as they performed 'Kids In America', 'Something About The Way You Look Tonight' and 'All You Need Is Love' – that last one was certainly an appropriate choice as the girls really were beginning to swoon.

However, now that the performances were going out live, the strain was beginning to tell. Harry was starting to get so nervous that he threw up in a corridor before going out on-stage. He also started having panic attacks, which became so serious he had to start doing breathing exercises to calm down, while drinking sparkling water to settle his stomach. There was talk of calling in the celebrity hypnotherapist Paul

McKenna to help him with his stage fright, and matters got so bad that Harry started vomiting up blood, necessitating a trip to the hospital. Happily, though, his nerves settled in due course.

Live television was something none of the boys had had any experience of, and having had to develop their act so quickly, without any of the touring and pratfalls that most bands get the chance to enjoy away from the public eye, it was hard. The boys were all still so young, and yet not only were they appearing and performing on national television, they were also becoming the focus of intense media interest. Even the most seasoned performer can find a huge amount of attention intrusive at times, and for four young boys, some of whom, Harry included, had only just left school, the whole experience was overwhelming. Harry knew he had to learn to cope; the stakes were so high that there was no going back now.

Nor were matters helped when various illnesses started to run rampant backstage. Niall developed laryngitis, various other contestants developed ailments and Simon Cowell himself felt so ill that he was unable to get out of bed, where he was said to be consuming honey and lemon, Angel's Delight and his mother's chicken soup. The fact remained that he wasn't there, though, and this meant he was missing valuable rehearsal time and mentoring opportunities, though his ex-girlfriend Sinitta was sent in to take his place.

Meanwhile, guest artists were appearing to give the contestants a taste of the real thing: if they got through, this is what might await them. Joe McElderry and Usher were on the first live results show; Diana Vickers and Katy Perry the second, followed by Cheryl Cole and Michael Bublé on the third. Rihanna, Bon Jovi and Jamiroquai made appearances in the fourth show; Shayne Ward and Kylie Minogue in the fifth; Take That, Westlife and JLS in the sixth and Olly Murs in the seventh. Justin Bieber, The Wanted and Nicole Scherzinger were there in the eighth week; the cast of Glee, Alexandra Burke and the Black Eyed Peas were in the semi-final; Rihanna and Christina Aguilera were in the first show of the finale and Take That were in the second. It was a starry crew. Although Harry and his band mates had no idea that they would soon be just as famous and sought after as these household names, they were certainly beginning to stand out. Brian Friedman, the show's choreographer, openly backed them to win, correctly identifying their growing appeal as a boy band. 'They signify what the charts are all about at the moment,' he told the *Daily Star*, adding presciently, 'They are young, good looking and can sing. You can just see mums and daughters all over the country falling in love with them.'

3

The Pressure Mounts

As the series moved on, the usual behind-the-scenes bickering between the judges – all of which was very good for ratings and drumming up publicity – began. Louis told Cheryl, 'It's not all about you.' Cheryl felt that Louis was 'a silly old man looking for attention'. Simon pointed out that Cheryl was looking 'less orange' than usual. Cheryl retorted that Simon's teeth were looking whiter than ever. Not to be outdone, the contestants also started feuding with one another: Katie Waissel landed herself in hot water after she hinted that she'd ended up in bed with the favourite to win the show, Matt Cardle, a story that was seen in many quarters as an attempt to maintain her position on the programme. Matt hotly disputed this, but Katie's ploy worked and she stayed in the show. None of it did anything to dint *The X Factor*'s popularity, although it created even greater bad feeling towards Katie, reinforcing her reputation for being highly manipulative.

Then there was seventeen-year-old Cher Lloyd, who was also making something of a name for herself. Rumours began to circulate that she and Harry, one year her junior, were getting close. The only surprise here, given Harry's subsequent relationships, was that she was only one year older than him, but his heart-throb qualities were already becoming clear; however the story managed to surface, it didn't hurt viewing figures. Whatever the truth about their relationship, the remaining acts were attracting more attention than ever: One Direction, Cher and Katie, along with the rest, nearly caused a riot when they went on a spending spree at Topshop and Top Man, invited by the owner Philip Green to kit themselves out, and more than forty security guards had to be brought in. In a sign that the pressure was really on, however, Katie fainted: it wasn't only Harry who seemed to be finding his new-found fame and celebrity a strain. That said, the group were also beginning to show signs that they quite enjoyed the attention, with reports that they were a little jealous to discover that the general hysteria was not just for them, but for their fellow contestants Matt, Aiden Grimshaw and John Adeleye, too.

Kerfuffles continued backstage. There were said to be rows about who was performing what, with Katie Waissell allegedly reluctant to sing the *Jungle Book* number 'I Wanna Be Like You'; Aiden Grimshaw, Wagner Carrilho and Matt Cardle apparently concerned that their songs made them look gay – they were asked to sing 'Diamonds Are Forever', 'Spice Up Your Life' and 'Baby One More Time' respectively – and One Direction equally unhappy with their number, 'Nobody Knows'. As always, however, all publicity is good publicity, and the boys seemed to be standing out more than ever.

Simon clearly realized One Direction's potential, whether or not they won *The X Factor*. 'The minute they stood there for the first time together – it was a weird feeling,' he told *Rolling Stone* many months later. 'They just looked like a group at that point. I had a good feeling, but then obviously we had about a five-week wait where they had to work together. They had to come back for another section of the show where they performed together as a group for the first time. I was concerned whether five weeks was long enough, but they came back five weeks later and were absolutely sensational.'

In these major reality talent shows, the big success story is not always the outright winner. It's often forgotten, for example, that Susan Boyle didn't actually win *Britain's Got Talent*, but instead was the runner-up. It was now becoming increasingly obvious that whatever the outcome of *The X Factor*, whether they turned out to be winners or not, One Direction had a serious career ahead of them. Although they had been a group for just a matter of months, they were already attracting their own fan base, with different fans for different members, and already Harry was starting to stand out amongst his peers. He was still struggling with nerves and stage fright, but the future was looking brighter by the minute, with enormous rewards on offer. All the boys were beginning to realize that a serious future in the music business could be on the cards.

Along with Matt Cardle, One Direction were strong contenders to win the show. Their female equivalents, Belle

Amie, had already been voted off, saving Katie Waissel in the process and making One Direction Simon Cowell's last remaining act. The canny Cowell stood to profit whatever the outcome, but it meant other people in the music industry were also taking an interest in the proceedings. By now the boys were beginning to enjoy themselves: the Halloween edition of the show had them dressed up as teenage vampires singing 'Total Eclipse Of The Heart'. And they also made their first ever red carpet appearance, in connection with another famous Harry, when they attended the premiere of *Harry Potter and the Deathly Hallows* together with Cher Lloyd. While they were slightly overshadowed by the stars of the film, especially Daniel Radcliffe, they still provoked a fair bit of screaming from their own fans. Emma Watson, it emerged, was hoping One Direction would win.

Already that strange transformation from entertainer to star was underway for all five of them, and the more famous they got, the more self-assured they became. Fame and success create a kind of virtuous circle: the more successful and famous a person is, the more famous and successful he or she becomes. It was now clear to everyone that the boys had a very bright future ahead, all that was left was to see how the competition would pan out. The boys themselves couldn't help but be a little bemused by all the attention, however, not least when a couple of fans asked them to sign their toenails, but they coped.

As with all things, though, there was a downside to the

fame they were all experiencing, and it was the female con-testants on the show who seemed to be feeling the strain most. Katie Waissel, who had become extremely unpopular in some quarters, told the *Daily Star* that she was increas-ingly nervous about going out in public: 'This is an intense situation to be in,' she said. 'I'm scared when I go out. I don't know what the reaction to me is going to be. We've all been out as a group and I do get worried that people are going to say something. At the end of the day I am a twenty-four-year-old girl, and to be booed publicly for, well, I don't know what for, it hurts. I was at rehearsals in Covent Garden the other day and someone threw a banana skin at me.'

Nor were the judges exempt from the pressure. Their bicker-ing continued, and however much it might have been staged, there was often an edge to their comments that implied they were getting genuinely tired of their peers. Matters weren't helped when contestant Treyc Cohen was sent off instead of the less talented Katie Waisell, who Cheryl had refused to nominate for the chop in a move seen as Cheryl protecting her own. It provoked an admonishment from Simon and more bad temper behind the scenes, but it also got a great deal of coverage in the media, with heavy criticism directed at Cheryl who, tough old showbiz stalwart though she may be, wouldn't have been human if it hadn't bothered her a little. Yet again there were accusations that the show was fixed, and yet again there was some serious bad feeling, along with all the hamming it up that everyone used to such good effect.

Did it really matter? Not a lot. If anything this was a lesson to Harry and his friends about how to generate publicity: Simon, Cheryl and the rest of them were past masters at manipulating the media, turning events to their advantage and generally getting their own way. Although Harry and some of his new friends had had a small amount of previous experience making music, none of them had seen the real world of show business up close before, and given the amount of attention they were about to receive, they were learning valuable lessons in how to cope. Not that they realized it at the time, however, for as the series progressed, with all its rows and infighting, the tensions grew greater as the stakes got higher.

Inevitably, there were rumours of friction within the band – hardly surprising, since the boys hadn't known each other at all just a few months earlier, but were now expected to pull together for the greater good. The closer they got to the final goalpost, the bigger the pressure upon them. They had entered the contest as complete unknowns, with very little to lose; now there was everything to play for, and it couldn't help but cause a strain.

The judges, ever conscious of the good television they were creating, continued to bicker amongst themselves. Cheryl threatened to refuse to vote if two of her acts were included in the sing-off, to which Simon retorted, 'Cheryl is a brat.' Then Louis joined in, deadpanning, 'Simon had a facial before the show and it's affected his brain.' Simon countered by calling Louis a 'rude pig', then Dannii went one better and asked Simon to name all the members of One Direction, something he failed to do. 'He doesn't even know the names of his own act,' gloated Louis.

The contestants and judges joined forces in combat when Wagner gave a somewhat unwise magazine interview, in which he described Cheryl as 'just a girl from a council estate who got lucky'. This provoked an aggressive on-screen confrontation with Cheryl, who was proud of her roots, as she informed Wagner. There was clearly no love lost between the pair, and the papers – and the public – lapped it up.

Even people who weren't involved in the show got caught up in the name-calling. Sir Elton John, never one to shy away from publicity himself, launched a public attack on *The X Factor*, saying it didn't prepare singers for stardom and was, 'boring, arse-paralysingly brain-crippling.' Never one to miss an opportunity for publicity themselves, the show's producers promptly dedicated the next episode to Sir Elton, getting the remaining contestants to sing some of his songs. The results, on the whole, were pretty atrocious, the great exception being One Direction, who did very well with 'Something About The Way You Look Tonight'.

As the show continued, so, too, did the drumming up of interest outside it. With the number of contestants whittled down to just sixteen, they paid a visit to Headley Court Military Hospital in Surrey, where men and women injured while fighting in Iraq and Afghanistan were being treated. All the contestants rose to the challenge, speaking warmly of the fighting spirit and determination these brave veterans were showing as they fought their way back to health. Katie, Matt, Cher and Zayn all spoke of their admiration for the invalids, and further goodwill was engendered when it turned out that all sixteen contestants would sing David Bowie's hit 'Heroes' on a charity single to benefit the Help for Heroes charity. The song was recorded in October, all sixteen finalists sang it on the 20 November results show, and the resulting single entered the UK and Irish charts at number one.

The next themed evening was devoted to Beatles' songs. Katie managed a fair rendition of 'Help!', Matt chipped in with 'Come Together', Cher sang 'Imagine' (not, technically, a Beatles song as it was John Lennon's creation after the group split) and One Direction kicked in with 'All You Need Is Love'. Paije Richardson was the unlucky one to be sent packing, while One Direction remained firmly in the game.

As the series progressed, so public interest in the contestants' backgrounds became more intense. One Direction would quickly have to get used to a great deal of public interest in their lives, but at least they weren't in Katie's position. Matters turned quite farcical when it was revealed that Katie's eighty-one-year-old grandmother, Sheila Vogel-Coupe, was not only a working girl in its most risqué sense, but also the star of a porn film. Katie was already under a great deal of pressure, and it was feared the news might tip her over the edge, although in truth she'd been at the forefront of so much publicity that one more crisis could hardly hurt.

What the boys in One Direction thought about it isn't on record, but they seemed pretty pleased with their lot, given that they were front-row guests at a fashion show for *very. co.uk*. There, they were more than happy to chat to the scantily clad models, especially Harry, who, in an early indication of his interest in the ladies, was seen chatting up one particularly pretty girl.

Katie and Wagner were the next to leave the show, an occasion Wagner marked by threatening to write a tell-all book about what really went on backstage. Further concerns were raised after some of the remaining contestants fell ill and were forced to miss the show. There were also fears that Cheryl might have had a relapse of the malaria that had plagued her earlier in the year. One Direction, however, had other things to worry about – namely that they might have been too successful for their own good. They had scored consistently well throughout, but that in itself might cause problems: 'The thing that always worries me is that it's easy for people at home to look at us and think, They're definitely safe because they haven't been in the bottom two, and that's not the case at all,' Louis fretted. 'It's clear with the people that have gone before that nobody's safe. It's been the most unpredictable year ever. People might sometimes see our young fans and think they don't need to vote. I just hope they do.'

One person who didn't seem that concerned was Simon Cowell. He had let it be known that whatever the outcome of the show he was planning on signing Matt, Rebecca Ferguson, Cher and One Direction, as his ex-girlfriend and long-term confidante Sinitta confirmed. 'Simon definitely wants to manage them,' she said. 'He knows they've got massive potential.' Simon also upset fans by publicly declaring that Cheryl should appear on Cher's debut album. If all this was aimed at drumming up interest, it was certainly working: in early December 2010, a record 20 million viewers tuned in to see Tesco worker Mary Byrne voted off the show. Meanwhile, the finals were approaching, and Cher, Matt, Rebecca and One Direction had all made it through.

Mary's departure was marked by some anger from the viewers, and from Mary herself, who didn't think she fitted the image Simon wanted to project. She had been an extremely popular contestant, a favourite with the viewers and one of the series' surprise hits. She was extremely upset about being voted off, and not at all averse to confirming the suspicions of some of the show's nay-sayers: 'It's not the show the public think it is,' she said in an interview with the *Mirror*.

'I knew the public had voted for me to stay on, and I actually thought the result would be based just on their vote. It was only on Saturday that I discovered there would be a sing-off where the judges decided. It's obvious Simon didn't want me in the final and I get that. I'm not as marketable to him as Cher, so he was never going to put me through. They fixed it for me to lose. It didn't matter what the public think.' In fact, it caused such ill feeling that Simon was forced to publish an open letter in a newspaper to refute the claims of fixing. The trouble with creating a monster, be it either a successful contestant or the show itself, is that it can sometimes veer out of control.

The interest from the public and the media was more intense than ever, and everyone involved was determined to make the most of it. Indeed, they were all hitting the publicity trail in their separate ways. Cher was pictured in tears after children from her old primary school gave her flowers and a good luck card, and she and Cheryl, who accompanied her, needed a police escort when they visited Malvern, Worcestershire. Meanwhile Matt performed a small gig at his local, The Five Bells in Colne Engaine, Colchester, and was mobbed.

All of this paled into insignificance, however, compared to the treatment meted out to One Direction. First they visited Harry's home town of Holmes Chapel, Cheshire; then they did an open air gig in Queen Square, Wolverhampton, Liam's home town. Such was the excitement generated within the 4,000-strong crowd that thirty-five people had to be treated for minor injuries – a sure sign, if any were needed, that the boys had cultivated a massive following and were going to become major stars.

Everyone involved with the show was pleased. Despite criticisms from the industry, especially from Sir Elton John, the series had generated a huge amount of interest and viewers, so the show's future seemed assured. 'If you think about music shows, it was all boring a couple of years ago,' Simon Cowell told the *Daily Express*. 'On our show, artists actually get to put on a show and I think that is really healthy. I have done my best to make the show more interesting every year. I would rather have controversy than be labelled boring and predictable. I don't even know if Cheryl, Dannii and Louis will be back next year. Everything gets refreshed and looked at again each year. I don't even know if I will be back – but *The X Factor* will.'

No one had done better out of the series than One Direction, though. They had already been spotted in Cowell's London offices, and at one stage during the proceedings he had commented, 'I would sign them now if that was an audition in my office.' He also appeared to like them on a personal level, remarking, 'They're polite to the crew. You can always tell what an artist is really like if they are polite off-camera and the way they treat the crew, the people around them, the fans. They're absolutely hilarious, nice people. I genuinely want them to win.' Or, to put it another way, they were already being superbly professional; they understood what was expected of them and realized that this was their big opportunity and that they mustn't blow it.

His fellow judge Louis clearly believed Cowell was planning their future, not least because they represented a great opening in the market – 'Of course we need another boy band,' he said. 'There's always room for boy bands and they are the perfect boy band. There's a whole new generation that are going to love One Direction. They're a young Westlife or Take That.'

As the hotly anticipated final approached, the drama continued behind the scenes. Cher, who appeared to have taken over Katie's role as resident drama queen, broke down at a press conference when she learned of a hate campaign against her, but appeared to be back to her usual perky self on her way to the final rehearsals. 'People keep telling me that I'm looking really happy this week and I think they're right,' she told the waiting reporters. 'I've got my sparkle back. I think it's because the stress has lifted. I know I'm not going to win so I'm so laidback about that. I've come as far as I wanted to and I'm very, very proud of myself. I think someone else deserves to win.' Diplomatic words indeed. One Direction, meanwhile, had been chosen to team up with Robbie Williams for the final – a sign, if ever there was one, of how highly they were being rated.

Cher was perhaps wise to pre-empt her departure as she was the first of the four finalists to leave the show in the live finals, vowing as she did so that she would make it on her own. All eyes were now on One Direction, who put in an extremely creditable performance of Elton John's 'Your Song', as well as duetting with Robbie on 'She's The One'. Simon attempted to quell speculation that a contract with his record label was already a done deal, saying that they still had to win the show if they were going to get on, but it was clear the band was on the verge of greater things.

Indeed, Simon was the first to contradict himself when the moment finally came. In the show's final, despite a heartfelt performance of Natalie Imbruglia's 'Torn' and a comment from Simon telling them they 'deserved to win', One Direction were the first to be voted off, with Matt Cardle as the ultimate winner. 'I am absolutely gutted for them. But this is just the beginning for these boys,' said Simon, seemingly forgetting his words of just a few days earlier. The boys themselves overcame their disappointment to acknowledge they had a future together: 'We are definitely going to stay together,' said Zayn. 'This is not the end.'

It certainly wasn't. For starters, Harry did win something: he topped a Brylcreem poll for 'best celebrity hair'. It turned out that One Direction ranked number three as the most talked-about celebrity newcomer of the year in research carried out by media agency PHD, which checks how much celebrities are mentioned on the net (Cher came first, followed by Matt).

Syco, Simon Cowell's management company, lost no time in signing the boys up to a £1.2 million deal. The band were summoned to his office. 'I've made a decision,' he told them gravely.

Zayn picked up the tale. 'There was a long, dramatic pause,' he said, 'at the end of which, he said he was going to sign us. Harry burst into tears and the rest of us had our heads in our hands.'

'It was what we wanted to hear more than anything else in the world,' Harry said.

And so, in the space of a few short months, their lives had been transformed. From total unknowns to household names, One Direction had found success faster than almost anyone involved in this type of reality show, with the possible exception of Susan Boyle. Like Susan, they hadn't won outright, but theirs was the career that would really take off and, like Susan, it wouldn't be long before they, too, found global fame. The boys were stars, separately and as a group. Very soon they were going to have the world at their feet. There would be hard work, rehearsals and a life open to public scrutiny, but the boys knew it was worth it. They were being given opportunities most people couldn't even dream of, and they weren't going to mess it up now.

It was an awesome prospect for anyone and something they couldn't be prepared for, no matter how hopeful they had been. From now on, the boys were going to have to learn even faster to keep pace with everything in their new lives, and this applied to Harry more than anyone. Still just sixteen and from a conventional Cheshire background, he was about to make the jump from schoolboy to superstar in a matter of months. So who, then, was Harry? And what had his life been like up until now?

4

A Star is Born

The day was 1 February, 1994, and in the charming village of Holmes Chapel in Cheshire, in the north of England, Anne Cox and Des Styles were jubilant. Anne had just given birth to their second child, a boy they called Harry Edward Styles, who was two years younger than his sister, Gemma. The family now seemed complete and settled back happily into its middle-class lifestyle, quite unaware that the boy who had just been born would one day become a superstar and one of the world's leading heart-throbs. Harry grew into a very appealing toddler: pictures of the time illustrate a little boy full of life and vitality, with a cheeky grin and big eyes. Nor was there any sign of his famous hair – the young Harry had blondish-brown hair, cut into a pudding-basin style, rather than the famous barnet that would one day set him apart from the crowd.

The young Harry had a slightly unusual attribute: four nipples. He had two that were normal size and two tiny ones further down his chest. However, in all other respects, everything was as you would expect: he grew quickly, got on well with Gemma, developed a series of favourite toys, including a teddy bear, and became the light of both his parents' eyes. In the background, however, all was not quite well. Anne and Des had started to grow apart and there were signs that the marriage wouldn't last. Harry, sadly, was going to come from a broken home.

Nevertheless, his earliest childhood was spent with both parents. Initially, home life was traditional: Des worked as a sales and marketing director and Anne was an office worker, and the children grew up in a comfortable middle-class household. According to his father, Harry's favourite food as a child was small tins of mandarin orange segments, and as Harry got older he became a very proficient cook, to say nothing of harbouring a healthy appetite.

Harry's first school was called Happy Days, a suitable name for someone of his sunny disposition, and Harry still has many happy memories of the place. He was already beginning to show signs of the considerable charm that would take him far. 'I got on really well with my pre-school teacher,' he once confessed, ''cause she was also my babysitter, so I think I got all the good toys first.' In truth, Harry was such a profoundly likeable child it's no wonder his teachers warmed to him. He got on well with his fellow pupils, too, finding it easy to make friends. Tellingly, Harry also found it easy to make friends with the girls – he wasn't one of those little boys who's interested only in playing with his own sex.

There were even some early signs of what was to come, since as a child, Harry was extremely musical. He adored Elvis Presley, whose recordings he was introduced to by his

How it all began . . . *X Factor* hopefuls One Direction pose
with their mentor, Simon Cowell.

Rumours that Harry was dating fellow contestant Cher Lloyd
turned out to be false, but they're still close friends.

The paparazzi soon closed in as Harry began to experience the less glamorous side of stardom.

Mobbed by adoring girls, Harry and the boys have often needed the services of security guards.

On the red carpet at the *Narnia* premier, while still on the *X Factor* –
the boys knew where they belonged.

Harry looks at home in the kitchen on *This Morning*.
He's a modern man who admits to loving cooking and cleaning!

The boys are excited to begin their tour and launch their first single,
'What Makes You Beautiful'.

In the lap of luxury . . . but Harry loves to play the clown!

Spotlight on Harry – the girls soon pick Harry out as their favourite 1D member.

When reports surface about Harry and Caroline Flack (fifteen years his senior), she is hounded by the press and angry Twitter trolls.

What a doll . . . but the other lads say it looks like Susan Boyle!

Thoughtful Harry buys the gang coffees all round.

Harry looks suave at the Brit Awards in his oversized bow tie.

Yes, it's real! The stunned group clutch their Brit award.

Living while they're young, the boys from One Direction
are set to take on the world!

father, and would play his music around the house, confessing that his favourite song was 'The Girl Of My Best Friend'. This interest only intensified when his father, grandfather and cousin clubbed together to buy him a karaoke machine, giving Harry lots of opportunity to sing around the house. He also loved The Beatles – one day the hysteria surrounding One Direction would be compared to Beatlemania – and was always encouraged to sing by his family. That karaoke machine was in many ways a form of early rehearsals: while Harry was just having fun, with no thought that this hobby would ever turn professional, he was nonetheless getting better all the time at what he did. Not only was he developing his singing voice, he was learning to perform, something that was going to stand him in remarkably good stead in the future. Other aspects of his musical personality also began to emerge, such as his little known talent for playing the kazoo.

From a very early age, it was apparent that Harry had an eye for the girls. At the age of six he became great friends with another six-year-old called Phoebe Fox, the daughter of one of Harry's mother's closest friends. 'I bought her a teddy bear the same as my one,' Harry told the *Sun*. 'She was the cutest little girl.' He was the cutest little boy, too, cultivating his toddler lady friends and proving quite a hit in the school playground. It was no surprise in later life that girls – and women – flocked to him, as Harry has a huge amount of natural charm.

Harry was also a big animal lover, and his first pet was

a dog called Max (a later pet was a hamster with the original name of Hamster). He continued to have a fairly normal childhood, developing other skills such as juggling and knitting, and progressing happily at school. In all, life was pretty happy – until, finally, disaster struck.

At the age of seven, Anne and Des announced they were getting a divorce. 'That was quite a weird time,' Harry later told the *Sun*. 'I remember crying about it. I didn't really get what was going on properly; I was just sad that my parents wouldn't be together any more.' In actual fact, Harry was devastated. He and Gemma were still so young – Gemma was just nine – and both were close to their parents. The family had seemed relatively happy, in as much as they could be – Harry was getting on well at school and had lots of friends – so why did there have to be this seismic shift inside the family home?

It was a shattering experience for everyone, and although the children remained close to both parents, life as they knew it was about to change for good, and nothing was ever quite the same again. Divorce scars children, and while it might be taking it a little far to suggest that Harry's attraction for older women stems from his parents' split and a need, in some way, to be mothered, it is possible the two are related. At any rate, it certainly shattered the illusion that they were a conventional happy family and Harry was devastated.

Des later confessed that the episode haunts him still. 'He was only about seven when I sat them down and told them I was leaving,' he told the *Daily Record*. 'Everybody was in tears. We were sitting in the lounge. Gemma and Harry were sitting on the floor in front of us, Anne and I on the sofa, and both of them were crying. Generally, you wouldn't see him cry as much as maybe some kids do – he wasn't generally emotional or a cry-baby – but he cried then. The way we sat them down and told them we weren't going to be together any more, it was probably the worst day of my life.'

It wasn't too happy for Harry and Gemma, either. The children were so distressed by their parents' break-up that Anne and Des attempted to repair matters, but in the end Des finally moved out. He was keen to put it on the record, though, that he remained a responsible father, staying in touch with the children, seeing them regularly and providing for them financially. It was just that he could no longer stay married to his wife. Anne felt the same and it was a mutual decision. The marriage simply couldn't go on any longer.

'I didn't just leave, it was a decision we should split,' Des told the *Daily Record*, in the wake of his son becoming a global phenomenon. 'Things weren't good for a while and it was the best way forward. At the time, everybody was in tears but children are very resilient. Of course, I missed him and Gemma, as you would unless you were some sort of monster. It was tough. I used to feed him every night at half ten, change his nappy, put him to bed when he was a baby and then I was no longer living with them. I used to see Harry and his sister Gemma every couple of weeks, I've always supported them financially and, when I can, emotionally. I'm not an estranged dad. It was a tough time to leave them but these things happen.'

It was certainly a time of upheaval. The family left Holmes Chapel and moved out into the Cheshire countryside, which only increased the sense for Harry that everything was changing, and not for the better. That he was attacked by a goat at the tender age of ten can't have helped either – in fact, it's made him nervous around goats to this day – and the family had a difficult couple of years until the flack settled and they were able to be happy together once again. One positive was that Harry's relationship with his mother became closer than ever. Now probably the best known of the One Direction mothers, not least because she's an active Twitter user, Anne was keen to encourage her son, shield him as much as she could from the ramifications of the divorce and build him up to be a man. She encouraged his ambitions, gave him confidence and fought to make sure he wouldn't be damaged by what had happened. The two of them grew ever closer, with Harry in turn giving his mother emotional support when she needed it.

When Harry was twelve, his life began to change once more, and this time for the better. For a start, they moved back to Holmes Chapel, much to the relief of the rest of the family. Secondly, Anne met Robin Twist, the man she would eventually marry and who became Harry's stepfather. Harry got on with Robin from the start and was very pleased when the marriage took place. Harry also acquired a girlfriend of sorts, despite his tender years, a girl by the name of Emilie, followed by another girlfriend called Abi, and he had his first kiss at the age of eleven.

Harry attended Holmes Chapel Comprehensive School, a local secondary school and sixth form centre with a wide catchment area that encompasses a wealthy part of Cheshire. Harry was a popular student, albeit a little boisterous, and he developed a habit of mooning, sometimes wearing a thong and sometimes not, which gave him a taste for going naked that is still very evident to this day. As his home life became more settled, the unhappiness of his parents' divorce retreated into the background, giving him time to build up the rest of his life. He was also a talented footballer, playing in goal for a local side, with his loyal mother turning out every Sunday to stand on the touchline in the freezing cold to support him.

Harry was particularly popular among the girls at school, something he later attributed to the ease he feels in the company of women. 'I have a lot of friends from school who are girls. And I grew up with my mum, Anne, and my older sister, Gemma, so maybe it comes from that. It's very natural and I've never been awkward around women,' he told the *Sun*. Pictures of him at his school prom showed him surrounded by girls, posing happily for a whole succession of them, utterly relaxed in female company, so perhaps it's no surprise that Harry has turned out to be the most popular member of One Direction.

The young Harry could also be a bit of a handful. One of his close friends, Will Sweeney, told the *Sun* that the two of them would run riot in the local supermarket: 'We'd act like complete idiots in public,' he recalled. 'Harry would go into

Tesco, pretend he had Tourette's and walk around screaming and shouting. We'd throw things at each other, we'd just create chaos and a bit of a mess. We were told off by security and customers. We played this game where you pick something up and launch it over your head without knowing where the other person is – and they've got to try to catch it. We grabbed all sorts – bread, sauces – and Harry dropped stuff everywhere. Harry and I got told off at Waitrose once because we were screaming, "Bogies!" as loud as we could. We would each scream, "Bogies!" louder than the other person; we would shriek until we were blue in the face. Harry loved it. He was always up for fun, wacky things, having a laugh, and he never cared what people thought.'

However, he could also be an extremely thoughtful son. 'Harry's a very romantic guy,' his mother told *Teen Now*. 'If I'd had a particularly bad day at work I'd come home to find he'd run me a bath and surrounded it with candles and even cooked me a meal. He just used to usher me out of the kitchen and say he'd got it all under control.' As well as being solicitous towards his mother, Harry was, by now, an accomplished cook, counting it as one of his hobbies, alongside badminton, which he played in his spare time.

In the background, Des was also keeping an eye on his son, performing the duties fathers traditionally do. 'I never needed to sit him down and tell him about the birds and the bees. I tried to train him up as we went along,' Des told the *Daily Record*. 'We had those conversations and it was almost as though he'd say, "Yeah, Dad, I'm on board with that," rather than going all sicky and saying, "Oh, Dad, don't talk about things like that," you know, the way some kids do.'

Harry's first proper relationship came about when he was fifteen. The lucky girl was called Felicity Skinner, and she became the object of much curiosity and envy when her beau achieved global fame. A pretty, perky blonde, Felicity even found herself followed on Twitter by One Direction fans, even though she hadn't seen Harry for some years.

'He was a really good boyfriend, very romantic and, yes, shy,' Felicity later told the *People*. 'He was good looking and obviously I found him very attractive. We were together for just under a year. A friend of mine called Liv introduced us. She lived where Harry comes from. It was a long-distance relationship but it was a lot of fun. We just clicked straight away and got on really well. He has a really cute smile. We started seeing each other when we were both about fifteen. He was really sweet. It was puppy love and we were definitely each other's first loves.'

The relationship didn't last, though. Apart from the problem of it being conducted long distance, the two of them were awfully young, with their futures stretching out ahead of them. Nonetheless, the fact that it lasted as long as it did was indicative of a certain amount of emotional maturity on Harry's part, which of course has surfaced again with his penchant for dating older women. In a sign of things to come, Harry also used to sing to her, which meant Felicity had at least some hint of what he wanted from life.

'There was no real reason why we split up,' Felicity later

recalled. 'We just drifted apart. I don't think the distance helped and we were really young. It was sad when we first broke up, but I'm happy now. When Harry became famous I thought it was weird because I knew him before all this happened and we'd been boyfriend and girlfriend. But I don't really think about it any more. I think it's funny when I hear Harry on the radio, and especially when a One Direction song comes on. I'm used to it now and I'm really proud of him. People always say I was lucky to have gone out with him, but I think he was the lucky one. We stayed in touch right up until a week before judges' houses. Then we didn't speak again.'

In the meantime, Harry had embarked on an extra-curricular activity that was going to stand him in good stead. One Direction wasn't Harry's first band. Initially, he supplied lead vocals for the band White Eskimo, which his friend Will Sweeny is still a member of; they entered a Battle of the Bands competition when they were in Year 10 and won. They began performing locally, and footage still exists on YouTube of Harry and the boys as he started learning his trade. While clearly an amateur, Harry nevertheless stands out, and the experience was hugely beneficial when it came to performing for a wider audience. Despite the intensity of his stage fright during the making of *The X Factor*, Harry had in fact been performing since his mid-teens.

At that stage, however, there didn't seem much genuine prospect of a music-making career. School still featured largely in his life and, like many people, Harry took on a part-time job, working in W. Mandeville Bakery in Holmes Chapel. Here he turned out to be as popular as he had been everywhere else, quickly becoming a much-valued member of staff. And, as has often been the case, he was particularly popular with the girls.

'He was the most polite member of staff we've ever had, customers really took a shine to him,' his old boss, Simon Wakefield, told *Heat* magazine. 'The shop suddenly had an influx of girls when Harry worked there, sometimes there'd be twelve pouring in at one time. Even now, a group of twenty girls will come in and start taking photos of the shop. He had a laid-back approach, which the girls loved. It's his husky voice that appeals to women and he has this incredible charm about him.'

But Harry wasn't just there to charm the girls; he also showed signs of the work ethic that's essential if you're to succeed in show business. There might not seem to be much in common between working part-time in a bakery and being a pop star, but Harry brought the same attitude to both. He wasn't a shirker, he was prepared to put in the hours and he quickly made himself indispensable about the place.

'He was a really hard worker,' Simon Wakefield revealed. 'His jobs were serving in the shop, cleaning the back, scrubbing the floor, washing the trays and cleaning the counter. Mopping the floor was his worst job, but I never heard him moan. He likes his food. He'd eat our special brunch pasties, which are bacon, beans, sausage and cheese. Every morning he'd make himself a big mug of tea and go for one of the big brunch pasties. Then he'd finish with either a vanilla custard slice or a millionaire's shortbread. When we had no customers, it was funny, because he'd break into song in front of all the staff. So we always knew he had it in him, we got used to it. It wasn't even round the back, it was in the front.'

Singing was becoming a recurring theme. Everywhere Harry went, he would sing. Whether it was to his girlfriend, or at work, or in his leisure time with his band, music was a fundamentally important part of his life. And not only did he have a good singing voice, he had something equally important in a star: charisma. When Harry was on stage, even in those very early days with White Eskimo, he became the focal point. All eyes were drawn to Harry, which was why, even back then, you could have predicted he was going to be a success.

And that success was getting closer all the time, although Harry was still living at home at this stage. After Gemma left home to go to university, Harry and his mother became even closer. 'It was just the two of us,' Anne told *Teen Now*. 'I went through a very hard time when his sister left for university – it was like I was going through empty nest syndrome. I was alone in the house with Harry for a year so we got even closer.' Robin was still around, of course, but it was a time of transition, as the children grew up and prepared to leave.

In Harry's case, it wasn't entirely clear what the future would bring. At the age of sixteen he took his GCSEs, and although he had by now realized he wanted a career in music, he was also realistic enough to know that the music world can be extremely precarious and that it might be an idea to have something to fall back on, which is why he started thinking about taking A levels in law, sociology and business. In the event, though, fate intervened before he got the chance.

There were other elements at work, too. Harry was getting restless and when he described Holmes Chapel as 'quite picturesque but quite boring', it became clear that he was seeking wider horizons. Rural Cheshire is extremely picturesque, but it's not the right setting for a boy who wants to spread his wings and become a pop star. If Harry really wanted to make his mark on the wider world, he was going to have to move.

It was around this time that he decided to have a go at auditioning for *The X Factor*, but even that wasn't straightforward. Harry was, after all, in a band, and if he was to take his chances alone, he was going to have to leave White Eskimo, temporarily at least. He did so, and while the band didn't split up, they were somewhat sidelined as Harry took his first faltering steps towards his new career.

Everyone was supportive. Harry's mother had always supported her boy in whatever he did, but this was a big step: a tryout in the world of show business. Harry was an extremely appealing and talented young man, but even so, what would happen if he didn't do well? Would the disappointment be too much for him? Just how would he deal with the stress?

In the event, Harry nearly found out what would happen if he didn't do well, for it was only the last-minute decision to take five solo singers and turn them into One Direction that saved him. After suffering from the most terrible stage fright, he also discovered how difficult dealing with stress could be. What was about to happen to him was beyond his wildest dreams. Even when Harry and the boys found out they were going to be made into a group, and even when they discovered they were to be signed on to Simon Cowell's record label, they couldn't have had a clue what was going to happen next.

One Direction have been compared to The Beatles, something Harry sensibly said was 'silly', but in one respect there is a similarity, and that's in the amount of attention they were about to receive. For the boys – all of them – were about to become a sensation, breaking America, gaining global recognition and turning into household names almost overnight. No one enjoyed the ride more than Harry, and equally, no one enjoyed the perks more, not least having an active love life. Harry had always liked women, and he'd never had any trouble attracting them, but his past life couldn't even begin to compare with what came next.

5

The Boys Strike Out

And so the deed was done. It had been a good
X Factor for Simon Cowell: as well as signing the
winner, Matt Cardle, to his record label Syco, he
had also offered contracts to Rebecca Ferguson,
Cher Lloyd and, of course, One Direction. The boys had
already garnered a huge amount of attention by appearing on
the televisions series; now all that was needed was to turn
them into stars.

There was serious money at stake, too. While each of the
boys was reportedly paid only a mere £8,000, the deal as a
whole was worth about £2 million. Even for the hugely
wealthy Cowell that was quite an investment, on top of which
there was a desire to strike while the iron was hot. The boys
might only have come third on the show, but they'd had the
lion's share of attention, and everyone wanted to cash in on
that before their new-found following forgot them. Not that
there was much chance of that. The industry was pretty much
in agreement that they were major new stars with a huge
future ahead of them. It was just the details that needed to be
planned.

The boys flew to the United States to meet with producers and songwriters – they would be working with the producer RedOne, along with Carl Falk, Savan Kotecha, Steve Mac and Rami Yacoub. In actual fact, no music would appear until the autumn, but that just helped the anticipation to build up. In the meantime, a book came out detailing their lives to date called *One Direction: Forever Young: Our Official X Factor Story*, which went straight to the top of the *Sunday Times* bestseller list. They were name-checked by Ant and Dec ('I loved playing the teenager,' said Ant of a sketch the duo did. 'I felt like I was in One Direction!') which, given that they had yet to release a single or even embark on *The X Factor* tour, was some indication of how fast and how far they had come. On their return from LA, they were mobbed at Heathrow airport, and there were reports that Comic Relief had approached them to record that year's charity single. In the event, that honour went to The Wanted, amid reports that Cowell was concerned it wasn't the right next step.

There was a taste of what was to come in February 2011, when *The X Factor*'s fifty-one-gig tour kicked off in Birmingham. Matt, Rebecca, Cher and Wagner all received an enthusiastic reception, as did Aiden Grimshaw, Paije Richardson, Katie Waissel and Mary Byrne, but it was nothing compared to the screaming that began when One Direction appeared. The boys were indisputably the stars of the show and overshadowed all the other acts. Matt might have been the outright winner, but he couldn't compete with Harry, Niall, Liam, Zayn and Louis, all of whom appeared to be coping remarkably well with their new-found fame. Any lingering doubts about the boys' star quality promptly vanished the minute the tour started and it became clear that they were a sensation. Simon Cowell had realized the boys were a good commercial prospect, but even he hadn't expected this reaction.

It might as well have been *their* tour, and the reviewers thought so, too. 'The main draw for the girl-dominated crowd was Cowell-mentored boy band One Direction,' wrote Michael Hogan in the *Daily Telegraph*. 'Hysterical screams greeted their every move. Hyperventilating ensued when they ran through the crowd. When cheekily cherubic heart-throb Harry Styles danced to the front, squeals reached fever pitch. The merchandise sellers knew their market – judging by their stalls, you'd think this was a One Direction concert.' And indeed you would.

'*The X Factor* 2011 live tour kicked off in style last night as the top nine finalists of last year's competition played their first dates at a full Birmingham's NIA. Matt Cardle showed why he won the competition with some spine-tingling renditions of tracks he performed on the show, but the biggest screams of the night were reserved for a certain five-piece boy group . . .' reported the website *TellyMix*. 'One Direction certainly stole the show, performing a selection of their most popular performances from last year's live show, as well as a special treat for fans – their cover of "Forever Young". It was the first time that the group had performed their planned winner's single live after they were eliminated third in last year's final.' This was the single they would have released had they won.

In total, the boys sang five songs: 'Only Girl', 'Chasing Cars', 'Kids In America', 'My Life Would Suck Without You' and 'Forever Young' – the only other contestants allowed five songs were Matt and Rebecca – but even then, the audience sometimes seemed on the verge of impatience when anyone other than the boys were on stage.

In the first of many reports about the boys' love lives, it emerged that twenty-four-year-old Rebecca Ferguson and eighteen-year-old Zayn Malik had become a couple, although it wouldn't last (and didn't raise eyebrows in anything like the same way as Harry's relationship with Caroline Flack). In the meantime, the hysteria surrounding the boys continued to grow: during the concerts the noise from the audience when they appeared on stage was so deafening it was sometimes difficult to hear them at all. Behind the scenes, plans continued for their recording debut, and in April, when the tour came to an end, those plans came to fruition. One Direction jetted off to Stockholm and Los Angeles, before returning to the UK, busy getting the album in the bag.

The fans clearly couldn't wait: their debut single 'What Makes You Beautiful' was the most pre-ordered Sony Music Entertainment single in history, which is saying something, given that other artists signed to the label include Michael Jackson, Beyoncé and Christina Aguilera, while Simon Cowell's right-hand man, Sonny Takhar, confidently predicted their debut album, *Up All Night*, would be one of the best pop records Sony had ever made.

The boys certainly weren't short of adventures as they got used to their new life. In Los Angeles to film a video to go with the single, Louis Tomlinson was stopped by the police because he was driving so badly. 'I got pulled over by the US police,' he told the *Sun*. 'They thought I was all over the place. The officer goes, "Listen, man, I can shut this thing down if you carry on driving like this. You're driving like a maniac." And I was like, "Man, put the gun down. I don't want no trouble."'

Unsurprisingly, perhaps, it was Harry who was being the most outrageous and getting all the girls. First, he stripped off in the plane's first class cabin on the way to LA, and then, during a day off at Santa Monica pier, he was spotted cavorting with various girls. 'The girls are lovely,' he confided. 'We took them out to a little fairground on the pier in Santa Monica to get to know them. We did the spinning teacups.' There were also rumours that Harry had got particularly close to one of the girls, Madison, appearing in the video, all of which helped give an early indication that Harry was quite the ladies' man. 'Harry and Madison were inseparable,' a source on the shoot told the *Sun*. 'They really hit it off and all the other boys kept teasing them both. They exchanged numbers and arranged to meet up when Harry is next in LA.' He was also spotted skinny dipping, but he got away with all of it, not least because of his considerable charm.

Harry took it all in his stride. 'I'm a seventeen-year-old boy, so I like girls,' he told *We Love Pop* magazine, 'but I prefer having a girlfriend. I like having someone I can spoil. Somebody to call up in the middle of the night and just talk to. I like getting close to someone like that.'

Harry was still getting used to the fact that absolutely everything he did got huge amounts of attention, from what he was wearing to whose phone number he was chasing. It was a lot to take on board in what had been a very short time. *The Magazine* asked him if he was getting a little bored of being famous: 'No, because I know I miss it the second I get to go home for a day,' he replied honestly. 'There's a lot of pressure to be a good role model, and people are keen to pigeonhole you as soon as you give them something to work with.' It was fortunate he took such a grounded attitude, because the boys' fame just continued to grow. Excitement was mounting in the run-up to the launch of the new single, a launch that would catapult the five of them to even greater fame than they'd so far experienced and, of course, even more attention.

In the summer of 2011, Zayn and Rebecca split up, claiming the pressures of their careers had driven them apart. Rebecca had been the subject of a great deal of abuse from One Direction fans, just as Harry's amours would later be, but everyone involved point-blank denied that was the reason for the split. The boys were just so sought after now that they couldn't open a door without causing a riot, on top of which there were rumours, all hotly denied, that Zayn had come under pressure *not* to have a girlfriend at the time their first single was released. It subsequently emerged that Louis had also split up from his girlfriend of two years, Hannah Walker. Again, the pressure of work was blamed. Harry had already admitted that they'd been discouraged from having girlfriends when they were in *The X Factor* house, but what about now? If anything, the boys seemed to want to make up for lost time.

The publicity machine was cranking up before their single's release. The boys gave their first television interview to Alan Carr, after which they started trooping around the showbiz desks of the nation's newspapers. Fellow *X Factor* finalist Cher Lloyd had already had some success with her single 'Swagger Jagger', which had gone to number one, and nothing less was expected of One Direction. There wasn't much doubt that their debut would be a major success, but the boys and their management were starting to think longer term – no one wanted the band to be a one-hit wonder, and there were plans to make them into the most successful act *The X Factor* had ever produced. There was praise from other people in the music industry, too, not least from those who'd helped prepare them: 'They're young, like when we started, so it makes me feel old. But it's a compliment to us if people think they sound like early McFly,' said McFly drummer Harry Judd. 'I wish we had their new single for ourselves – it's fresh.'

McFly singer Tom Fletcher added: 'They're a really like-able bunch of guys and they've got everything it takes to hit the big time. They've recorded a song I wrote for them – I just hope they use it.'

There were fresh waves of hysteria when the video for the single was released, so much so that extra bodyguards had to be employed when they made a promotional trip to Ireland. The boys continued to tease in the media: Harry told the *Sun* that he was single, saying, 'I like cute girls who are funny. I don't really have a type but I do like girls with short hair . . . but I also like girls with long hair.' Harry liked girls, point blank – there was no doubt about that.

All the boys liked girls, but they were beginning to notice who seemed to go down best. 'He has all the power in his curls,' Niall said of Harry. 'The women love him. And he loves getting naked. He's always in his boxers.' Women were regularly throwing themselves at him: one fan, who was old enough to have known better, attempted to get Harry to autograph her breasts. He refused.

The boys were also getting used to mixing in showbiz circles. They were spotted at Alexandra Burke's birthday party in the fashionable London restaurant Gilgamesh: the word at the time was that their management weren't too pleased about it and sent in minders to bring them out. The boys responded by hiding in the loos. On another occasion they attended a charity auction at London's famous Savoy Hotel, during which Harry bid £7,000 for two tickets to the UK Grand Prix. Meanwhile, the hysteria continued, despite the fact that they had yet to release a single. It was partly about creating a buzz, of course, but if they got this much attention before they'd even made a record, what was it going to be like when the single was released? The boys could have been for-given for being nervous, but in actual fact they were all enjoying themselves too much.

All along, Harry maintained his sense of humour. Going on Radio 2, he claimed that the band were paid in cola bottle sweets. And what, he was asked, would happen if their single did well? 'It might go up to higher stakes,' he replied. 'Maybe chocolate bars' – it would have taken a lot of chocolate bars to get those Grand Prix tickets.

As the pre-publicity for the single continued, the boys were asked who they had a crush on. Niall opted for Kate Middleton, Louis went for Natalie Portman, Liam chose Leona Lewis, while Zayn favoured Jessica Alba. And Harry? 'Caroline Flack is absolutely gorgeous,' he said.

Meanwhile, they continued to garner praise from estab-lished stars. Ronan Keating was one: 'They have a great machine behind them and are going to be superstars,' the Boyzone star told the *Sun*. 'They are going to be the biggest band this country has seen, although maybe not as big as Take That.' Some people thought differently, though, and were beginning to compare them to Take That – possibly the best-loved band in Britain and bordering on national treas-ures. It was high praise indeed.

The boys themselves were well aware of how lucky they would be to tread in those particular footsteps. 'The dream is to have a career like Take That's,' Harry told the *Daily Star Sunday*. 'Take That are in a league of their own; they are the ultimate boy band and have the career we wish for in our wildest dreams. We know it's early days, but we would love to be making music for as long as they have. Our dream would be to sell out eight days at Wembley like they did.' They might not have been there yet, but they were clearly determined to give it their all.

There was more whistle-stop touring of the country by helicopter as the release date of the single drew ever closer: 11 September 2011. The boys could hardly believe the fuss they were causing: 'We're five normal lads, we're not massively ripped, we don't have amazing bodies and we freely admit we can't dance,' Zayn told the *Sunday Mirror*. 'We had a girl who flew from Australia to America on her birthday just to meet us at the airport. Now that's utter dedication. It's unbelievable really.'

Niall added: 'You start to recognize the same girls because they turn up wherever we are, although there have been a few new ones recently. I've noticed a load from France. Maybe it's their school holidays or something.' Or maybe it was an indication of the band's global appeal. No one could ever predict which British stars would break the notoriously difficult American market, but given the fuss surrounding One Direction, it was looking like they stood a very good chance.

As the release date of the single loomed, Simon Cowell, the man ultimately in charge of orchestrating their careers, was attending to his television shows in the United States. He nevertheless maintained an extremely hands-on approach and was constantly in touch with his protégés to make sure everything was going according to plan. The boys were fulsome in their praise of him, announcing that he allowed them a great deal of freedom and say in what tracks would be included on the forthcoming album. They also joked that they weren't allowed to have his phone number on the grounds that they might inadvertently make it public. Still the publicity tour continued. They joined a star-studded fundraising day with City brokers, where that other famous Harry, Prince Harry, was also present, and rubbed shoulders with Princesses Beatrice and Eugenie, Kelly Brook, the Cheeky Girls and the London Mayor, Boris Johnson. They seemed entirely at home in such elevated circles, too.

As the material rewards began to emerge, the boys started settling into their own flats. Louis and Harry were the only ones to share, but both were delighted with their new place, which had its own cinema room. As well as being the most high-profile member of the group, Harry was also the youngest, so there was a sense that he needed to have an eye kept on him. In September, when the band celebrated Niall's eighteenth birthday, Harry quipped disconsolately that he would celebrate with a hot Ribena – legally, he was still too young to drink. When the boys appeared on *Daybreak*, they drank champagne to celebrate the occasion, while Harry nursed an orange juice.

Eventually the day came for the single to be released and within three days 'What Makes You Beautiful' had sold 100,000 copies. A great deal of thought and planning had gone into it, considering what was at stake: it was written by

Rami Yacoub, Carl Falk and Savan Kotecha, and was produced by Yacoub and Falk. Instrumentation was provided by Falk (guitar) and Yacoub (bass). Serban Ghenea handled the audio mixing, and Tom Coyne the audio mastering. John Hanes helmed the mix engineering, for which Phil Seaford served as the assistant, and it was recorded at Cosmos Studios and Kinglet Studios in Stockholm, Sweden. The accompanying music video, which went on to win three MTV Video Music Awards, including Best Pop Video, showed One Direction in Malibu and was directed by John Urbano.

One Direction all had a say in choosing 'What Makes You Beautiful' as their debut single, and they were all enormously relieved with the result. 'I think for us we wanted to release something that wasn't cheesy, but it was fun,' Harry told *MTV News*. 'It kind of represented us. I think it took us a while to find it but I think we found the right song.' His fellow band members agreed: when the stakes were this high, they had to get it right.

There was no doubt at all that the boys were going to have a number one. The hysteria was so bad now there was a serious danger of someone getting hurt – on one occasion, in Glasgow, the boys were leaving in a Mercedes van with blacked-out windows when fans managed to break through the police cordon and starting banging on the windows. The boys were notably astonished as their tour manager forced the girls to stand back so the car could move away. 'We never expect to see those kind of scenes or to hear the screams,' Harry told the *Sun*, but in truth it was commonplace now.

None of the boys had quite got used to the uproar they provoked, but it proved the point again and again: the boys had become massive stars. Fame had its limitations, though: the boys turned down all requests to turn on Christmas lights that year on the grounds that the security risks would be too high.

It was also becoming apparent that the fivesome had a seriously good chance of breaking the United States. The spectacular performance of the first single had made that clear, and the boys weren't being allowed to rest on their laurels – they were bundled off to New York to shoot their next video and schmooze record bosses under the guidance of Simon Cowell. Cowell himself was openly comparing them to Take That, a clear sign that he believed they could achieve even greater things, and it came as no surprise when it was announced that the single had gone to number one.

One person watching the proceedings with a jaundiced eye was the winner of *The X Factor*, Matt Cardle. He wasn't happy at all about what was going on and he wasn't afraid to say so. 'They're competition and it is s*** they got to release before the winner of the actual show,' he told the *Sunday Mirror*. 'It's also worrying me that if One Direction decide to get slicker and go for more of an older market, then I'm stuffed too. It shouldn't have happened really. Simon's naughty. I just hope I'll be able to cement myself into the charts before that happens. Otherwise I'll be fuming. I can't win unless I have an album that does the talking, and I think it does.'

In fairness, Cher had released a single before One

Direction, and done very well with it, but the truth was that Cowell had had a bumper year, finding several potential stars. Even he couldn't have forecast the kind of fuss that One Direction were inspiring – the boys were a sensation; they were so successful that they were causing talk of a boy-band renaissance.

In many ways, it was understandable that Matt was upset, because it wasn't just the fans who loved the new single, the critics were pretty taken with it, too. Ailbhe Malone of *NME* said the song would appeal to the teenage audience and that its chord progression was 'simple enough to be played on an acoustic guitar at a house party'. *Newsround* called it 'fun, upbeat and incredibly catchy', while *AllMusic*'s Matthew Chisling called it an 'effervescent and fresh tween love song'. Sophie Goddard from *Cosmopolitan* called the single 'ridiculously catchy' and *Student*'s Jack Murray rated 'What Makes You Beautiful' five out of five stars and called it 'not only the best pop single of the year so far, but potentially of any *X Factor* contestant ever'. Could it get any better?

Tanner Stransky of *Entertainment Weekly* awarded 'What Makes You Beautiful' a B+ grade, calling the song 'shallow but crushworthy' and making the point that boy bands are not dying out. Jason Lipshutz of *Billboard* called the song 'the real deal', and said that it is as 'endlessly playable' as 'N Sync's 'Bye Bye Bye': 'Easy to hear why this single has stuck. Like 'N Sync's most durable hits, with a cheeky electro-pop twist.'

Stephanie Abrahams of *TIME* understood exactly why the boys were so popular, adding 'The group takes cues from the boy bands of yesteryear with bubblegum lyrics about young love – "The way you flip your hair gets me overwhelmed" they croon in their breakout single – which any parent can get behind.' Robert Copsey of *Digital Spy* gave it four out of five stars, praising its catchy melody and saying it was 'adorable, completely innocent and bound to cause a stir amongst your mates', while Zachary Houle of *PopMatters* felt that it was a 'nice get-up-and-go dance number'.

'What Makes You Beautiful' won the BRIT Award for Best British Single at the 2012 Brit Awards, which was held on 21 February 2012. The song also won the Teen Choice Award for Choice Music: Love Song at the 2012 Teen Choice Awards. The band's success had been total: they had proved themselves to be one of the best acts to emerge from *The X Factor* and were now a serious force to be reckoned with in their own right. In less than a year they had gone from totally unknown to household names – and even greater triumphs lay ahead.

6

A Lot Like Life

The boys were now rarely out of the papers. Everything they did, from larking about while filming videos to their latest girlfriends – one by one the boys were getting loved up, and only Harry remained single – made the headlines. There was some hilarity when the official One Direction dolls went on sale, with many people good-naturedly informing Harry that his doll bore a distinct resemblance to Susan Boyle, but he took it in good stead. 'It's weird seeing dolls of yourself, but it's fun moving the body parts into cool positions,' Niall told the *Daily Star*. 'My doll would beat the others in a fight, but Harry's is the beefiest for some reason,' added Zane. The hysteria surrounding the band continued – the Radio 1 presenter Chris Moyles actually had to move his studio to a secret location, such were the concerns about security and besotted female fans storming the show.

Behind the scenes, though, One Direction were attracting some very different admirers: big business. It now seemed so certain that they would succeed in breaking the United States that American record-label executives were battling it out to sign them up: the main contenders were L. A. Reid of Epic, Rob Stringer of Columbia and Peter Edge of RCA. The band's manager, Richard Griffiths, was handling negotiations and the competition was intense. The boys themselves were delighted, even though they were on the opposite side of the Atlantic from the negotiations. For them, though, it was business as usual as a One Direction Nokia phone had just been launched by Carphone Warehouse.

As for the other *X Factor* contestants, Matt Cardle finally got to release the lead single from his debut album: a Gary Barlow-penned number called 'Run For Your Life'. Critics were divided about its merits, veering towards the negative, and it didn't do anything like as well as One Direction's offering, peaking at number six. Matt had been fairly good-hearted about the situation so far, but now something inside him appeared to snap. He gave an interview to *Look* magazine, in which he appeared highly critical of *The X Factor* and, by implication, Cowell: 'I massively compromised myself for *X Factor*,' he said. 'I wore yellow trousers and sang Katy Perry's "Firework", for fuck's sake. Singing pop songs without my guitar and covered in make-up didn't sit right. I hear people in the street saying, "There's the guy that won *X Factor*." I can't wait for that to just disappear.'

It was hard not to sympathize: Cardle had been comprehensively overshadowed by One Direction, who had got all the kudos, record sales and critical success. Then again, winning *The X Factor* guarantees nothing, as Matt, alas, was beginning to find out. One Direction, meanwhile, clearly had a very different relationship with Cowell, with Harry now claiming to be giving Simon relationship advice. Shortly afterwards he was pictured for the first time with Caroline Flack. Not only was Harry proving to be a ladies' man, he was also something of an agony uncle to the rest of the group, to say nothing of being a matchmaker. It was Harry who had introduced Louis to underwear model Eleanor Calder, who had become Louis's girlfriend.

In October 2011, the famous boy band Westlife broke up, prompting musings about the nature of modern boy bands and speculation as to who would take their crown. It was pretty obvious that One Direction was a serious contender, with a shelf life that seemed likely to extend far beyond that of many another boy bands. Somehow, the boys were managing to deal with what had become an increasingly pressurized situation without losing their cool: they remained as sunny and good-natured as ever, and nor did it seem to be going to their heads. It's often the case that people who are catapulted to fame from relative obscurity start to assume that the world owes them a living, but this was not the case for the members of One Direction.

While slightly stunned by what was happening to them, they all realized they were extremely lucky and that they mustn't take their new lives for granted. It could still all disappear overnight. In an interview with *The Sunday Times* – which seemed to point out that the boys appealed almost as much to fortysomething mothers as to their teenage offspring – Niall commented, 'We also feel that we are them [normal teenagers on the verge of adulthood] who have been given a massive opportunity.' It's an attitude that served them well.

Certainly, the boys' image was a subject for debate. All five let it be known that they had already lost their virginity, though they refused to go into greater detail – there were concerns that they should come across as, if not squeaky-clean, then certainly not too adult. Their management had forbidden them to do topless photo-shoots and they were encouraged to appear as normal as it is possible for world-famous, about-to-become-millionaire teenagers to be. The boys spoke a lot about being just like their fans: there were good commercial reasons for not letting success go to their heads.

Perhaps because of that squeaky-clean image there was widespread disgust when the forty-year-old comic David Walliams told Chris Moyles on the Channel 4 show *Quiz Night* that he liked Harry's hair and would like to perform a sex act on him (Walliams is straight). A number of disgusted viewers complained to Ofcom, as well they might. It was tot-ally out of keeping with One Direction's image as an innocent group: boys who were typical teenagers, liked girls and were still fresh-faced rather than experienced and worldly. Walliams 'joke' spoke of quite a different world.

In November, the band's debut album, *Up All Night*, was released. It was another critical and commercial success, top-ping the charts in sixteen countries and garnering widespread praise for its youthful appeal. It went in at number two in the UK album charts, becoming the UK's fastest-selling debut album in 2011, and went in at number one in the United States, making One Direction the first ever British group to have reached the US number one with a debut. 'By selecting a high calibre of songwriter, there's some nifty little tunes on here,' wrote the *Sun*, adding, 'There's only one direction this is going – straight to the very top.'

Other critics agreed. It has 'limitless potential for the time being, this is a perfectly sized, and targeted, collection', said *AllMusic*'s Matthew Chisling. It was a 'laudable addition to the boy-band pantheon,' said Zachary Houle of *PopMatters*, adding that it was a 'well-crafted slice of pop you can pop bubbles to'. It was 'a collection of pop rock with killer choruses', opined Robert Copsey of *Digital Spy* and 'an adorable as expected debut with a surprising amount of bite'. It was a collection of 'toe-tappers that are just impossible to dislike', said *Cosmopolitan*'s Sophie Goddard. And so it went on. There were, inevitably, a few dissenters, but the views of the majority were that the boys had lived up to expectations. This in itself, of course, created a further weight of expectation. Whilst previously they'd had nothing to compare themselves to, now their next album was going to have to be as good as the last.

And the same applied to their follow-up single, but when 'Gotta Be You' was released in November 2011 it, too, lived up to expectations. Written by August Rigo and Steve Mac, it peaked at number three, making it One Direction's second Top 10 hit, and again garnering good reviews from the critics, with Robert Copsey giving it four out of five stars. The

timing was relevant, too: it was out just in time for the lucra-
tive Christmas market, and much was made of the fact that
the newcomers were challenging established acts, such as
Michael Bublé, The Wanted, Justin Bieber and fellow former
X Factor stars, JLS.

It had been a full year now since the boys had come to
national attention on *The X Factor*, and they returned to the
scene of their triumph to perform with Lady Gaga as the
eighth series began to come to a close. All five of the boys
held her in some degree of respect, given the spectacular success she'd achieved since launching herself on an unsuspecting
world a couple of years earlier, and there was another connection, as One Direction had used her producer, RedOne,
on one of the tracks on their new album. 'RedOne will be a
talking point,' Harry told reporters backstage. 'He's told us
what she's like to work with, how professional and hardwork-
ing she is. And more importantly, that she's a really nice girl.'

As the boys became more of a fixture in the world of show
business, so they started appearing on the kinds of pro-
gramme that attract the great and good, such as Children In
Need, where they found themselves alongside Kylie Minogue,
Alesha Dixon, Fearne Cotton, Adele, Steps, Susan Boyle and
Sir Terry Wogan. As the *Daily Star Sunday* gave away signed
One Direction dolls, it was becoming quite difficult to
remember a time when the band didn't dominate Planet
Celeb. Meanwhile, rumours about Harry's relationship with
Caroline Flack started to emerge. Yes, the age gap raised eye-
brows, but there was now so much razzmatazz surrounding

the boys that Harry's burgeoning relationship only increased the already intense scrutiny the band were coming under. All five boys made it into the annual publication of *Tatler* magazine's Little Black Book, its round-up of the most eligible singletons in Britain, and the growing numbers of fans agreed.

After some intensive speculation, it was finally announced that One Direction had confirmed their US record deal: they signed with Columbia, which numbered Adele among its artists, as well as the likes of Bob Dylan, Bruce Springsteen and David Bowie. Behind all the public congratulations, there was some very hard-headed business going on: there was serious money to be made now and Columbia record bosses were determined to cash in. It wasn't a difficult decision to sign One Direction, according to Steve Barnett, co-chairman of Columbia: 'Other artists in that category had gotten a little older,' he said. 'I just thought there was a void and maybe they could seize and hold it.' A huge publicity campaign was planned, including a Facebook campaign to bring the boys over to the States, which attracted 50,000 members within days. It was pretty innovative stuff: while standard practise would have been to release a single and then bring the boys over for a tour, here social media was used to whip up interest in One Direction before a song or tour was announced. Fans were asked to sign petitions and enter video competitions to win a concert in their town – Dallas won – while membership soared to 400,000.

The boys were involved in other activities, too. The eighth

series of *The X Factor* had had a rather lacklustre reception: Simon Cowell was absent, which didn't help, and none of the acts had grabbed the public's imagination in the way that four of them had done the previous year. The finalists, once more, were going to join forces to release a charity single, but there were fears that this year they weren't going to generate enough interest to sell well. In the end, One Direction and JLS were co-opted on to the record – a cover version of Rose Royce's 'Wishing On A Star' – to raise money for the Together For Short Lives charity, which helps children who are unlikely to reach adulthood. The boys went on to visit Rainbows Children's Hospice, which was funded by the charity, and spoke about how moved they were to be able to help. All of this was encouraged by Simon Cowell who, of course, is far and away the biggest winner of *The X Factor*, and someone who's clearly determined to give something back himself.

With so much going on, it was becoming harder and harder to keep the boys' feet on the ground, although they did try. They were all still in touch with their pre-fame friends, although Harry was increasingly seen in celebrity circles, not only with Caroline, but also James Corden and Rio Ferdinand. He also started to find himself in a position whereby other celebrities wanted to meet him rather than vice versa – anyone pictured with Harry and the rest of the boys was certain to achieve blanket coverage in the press.

The boys were becoming aware of this. By this stage, if any of them was so much as pictured with a girl, it was assumed – sometimes rightly, sometimes wrongly – that she was a new girlfriend. This wasn't necessarily good for their image, and a lot of the time it wasn't actually true. They were at pains to emphasize that they were not ladies' men, but given the amount of attention they were getting – and Harry's relationship with Caroline, which was now an open secret – no one was buying it. They might, in their own words, be 'ordinary teenage boys', but they had found themselves in an extraordinary situation and could be forgiven for enjoying themselves at least some of the time.

To tie in with the new album, ITV2 screened a documentary, *One Direction: A Year in the Making*. It provided a behind-the-scenes glimpse into the boys' story, from coming third in *The X Factor* to achieving their current superstar status. The boys reflected on what had been a tumultuous year, and their growing astonishment at the fans' reactions as they jetted across Europe was plain for all to see.

Harry, of course, was loving every minute of it, and was beginning to be compared to a certain exceedingly famous rock star. It was the Rolling Stones' fiftieth anniversary, and while comparisons were being drawn between the world's greatest rock 'n' roll band – as the Stones like to style themselves – and relative newcomers such as One Direction, it was clear that Harry also had quite a bit in common with Stones frontman Mick Jagger. Quite apart from the fact that both have an eye for the ladies, there's a distinct physical resemblance. Both are lean and rangy, and while Mick is a somewhat grizzled specimen these days, Harry is still a fresh-faced youth who could just about pass for the younger

Rolling Stone. Both have a defining physical characteristic: in Mick's case it's his famous lips, and in Harry's it's his hair. It boded well for the younger star since Mick Jagger is possibly the most successful rock star the world has ever seen. If Harry could emulate even a fraction of his success, he had quite a career ahead of him. His fellow band mates even teased him about it, saying they'd bought Niall a life-size waxwork of Barack Obama (it's never been established if this is true) and that they would do the same for Harry with a waxwork of Mick.

Perhaps it was Harry's growing reputation as a ladies' man that prompted a certain famous vamp to speak out. Nancy Dell'Olio, who at fifty is probably a little old even for Harry, was at pains to stress that she now had a new set of admirers – the entire band. They had met up in Dublin when they stood outside her dressing room door: 'They seemed very fascinated,' Nancy told the *Sun*. 'They are going in the right direction if they are attracted to me. I am glad they are not interested in the likes of Cheryl Cole. To be with a mature person allows you to read books together and learn fast.' The boys didn't respond to this curious declaration, but to be singled out by Nancy Dell'Olio only emphasized that their appeal spread well beyond their own generation – as has been previously pointed out, mothers loved them, too.

As the finale of the latest series of *The X Factor* approached, the boys were again called upon to sprinkle some stardust across the television screen. They were part of a whole range of show-business heavyweights wheeled on for the occasion and were due to perform with Coldplay, Leona Lewis, Michael Bublé, JLS and Westlife. *The X Factor* bosses were determined to sign off the somewhat lacklustre series with a splash, and it was already being spoken of as one of the TV events of the year. *The X Factor* judges, Gary Barlow, Tulisa and Kelly Rowland, were all called upon to perform, too. In the event, girl band Little Mix won the show, the first group ever to do so, something that was given added piquancy because they'd been backed by One Direction. It was rumoured that band member Perrie Edwards had struck up a relationship with Zayn, and that was almost the first casualty of the win, as apparently Perrie promptly dropped him, saying she wanted to concentrate on her career.

Even so, the show was something of a disappointment. Despite its roster of stars, it dropped 3.5 million viewers from the previous year – Cowell's absence had clearly been felt – and was beaten by *Strictly Come Dancing*, prompting concerns for the show's future, not least from Cowell himself.

The boys had no worries, though; they were going from strength to strength as they set off on their first tour, with an opening night at Wolverhampton Civic Hall. This was their chance to start posting outrageous rock-star demands, but they kept it pretty simple, asking only for jelly babies, Haribo, clean pants and socks. When they arrived, they were delighted to discover that their dressing room contained a sauna and steam bath: 'That's it,' Louis told the *Sun*, 'before every gig we are having a sauna or bath together.' They certainly downed a few Haribo each before running out on stage: perhaps the sugar rush gave them the burst of energy they needed to delight their adoring fans.

The concert went down a treat. One Direction started with 'Na Na Na', the B-side of 'What Makes You Beautiful', followed by a mixture of songs from their album and numbers they had performed on *The X Factor*. Other numbers included Amy Winehouse's 'Valerie' and Kings of Leon's 'Use Somebody', as well as 'Gotta Be You' and 'One Thing', which was to be their next single. And, of course, there was 'What Makes You Beautiful', which provoked the biggest screams of the night.

It was all still a very new experience for the boys, and one way in which they coped was to imagine they were someone else. Louis told *Playlist*'s James Cabooter, 'When we are on stage sometimes we think we are someone else, or put ourselves in somebody else's shoes. Liam is a Take That boy. So he thinks he's Gary Barlow.' Liam added, 'When you see somebody do something on stage I'll replicate it and imagine I'm looking at me. It's weird. There's loads I steal from other people.' Harry wasn't to be left out either: 'I love Chris Martin. Sometimes I do his jig on stage,' he said. Actually, they were all emerging with distinct stage personas – clearly they felt they needed a mask to hide behind as they coped with their new-found fame.

The boys were also having to get used to life on the road. Any band that wants to go the distance has to put in a great deal of time touring, and One Direction were no exception. They were travelling around on a tour bus decorated with posters and pictures – Harry claimed to have a picture of Liam in his bunk; Louis countered that that was all right as Liam looked like a girl anyway – and living out of a suitcase. The bond between the five of them had become really strong, which was just as well: they were spending a huge amount of time in each other's company and any tensions would have been disastrous. The boys had one thing in common if nothing else: only they knew what it was like to have been plucked from obscurity and turned into a band called One Direction. The stresses and strains were the same for all of them, and if it ever felt too much, then at least they had each other to confide in. They certainly weren't living the lives of ordinary teenagers any more.

Harry continued to enjoy every minute. There was some amusement when it emerged that Harry was the new favourite name for baby boys in 2011, and, of course, he was in good company with a number of other famous Harrys, such as Prince Harry, Harry Potter and McFly drummer Harry Judd – somehow it felt as if Harry Styles was utterly at one with the zeitgeist. Harry was the name to have and Styles was one of the most high-profile Harry's of them all.

If there was a downside to any of the attention Harry received, it didn't so much affect him as his fans. Concern had already been voiced about the fact that Caroline Flack had received death threats after her relationship with Harry became public, and now something similar was happening to some of their fans. After One Direction posted an invitation on Twitter for girls to put themselves forward to be serenaded by the boys, twenty-year-old Hollie Gilbert was selected to be serenaded by Harry. This duly took place at their opening concert and almost immediately prompted ugly messages from internet trolls, including, 'I think you're pathetic,' and, 'You're not even pretty, why did Harry choose you?' (For the record, Hollie is very pretty, which might perhaps have prompted the jealousy.)

A couple of other girls were targeted, too, sparking so much concern amongst the band's management that the interactive part of the concert was scrapped. These were problems boy bands hadn't experienced before: while social networking had existed for some time, no one could have anticipated that a perfectly innocent request for fans to get in touch would spark such resentment elsewhere. An unpleasant minority – and it was only a tiny percentage of their fans – had managed to ruin it for everyone else; because after their nastiness no one, including the trolls themselves, was going to be singled out to be serenaded. Such are the travails of being a heart-throb in the digital age.

Another travail was that nothing remained private for long, although the boys did sometimes bring this on themselves. Harry and Louis held a boisterous New Year's Eve party at their shared flat: James Corden was present, as were an awful lot of girls. Harry was pictured with his arm around a blonde – Caroline was in India at the time, although Harry made a point of phoning her – and the pictures duly appeared in the media. The boys were unrepentant. 'Our New Year's Party was absolutely crazy!' tweeted Louis. There were, it seemed, benefits to being a pop star.

They took nothing for granted, though. On their way back from a concert, the boys and two crew members were all in their tour bus when it was rammed from behind by a car. Three of the band – Louis, Zayn and Niall – had to be treated for severe headaches, and police and ambulances were called to the scene. They'd all suffered a degree of whiplash and horrified fans were quick to respond to the news via Twitter. At first there were concerns that someone might have been fatally injured, but the boys, though shaken, had had a lucky escape.

There were subsequent concerns that the next concert, in Plymouth, might have to be cancelled, but the boys were having none of it. 'Don't worry, we're fine,' tweeted Niall. They knew the importance of keeping the show on the road and not letting their fans down. And so they took to the stage at Plymouth Pavilions, delighting the fans and proving conclusively that they were professionals who understood what was expected of them. It was quite a start to 2012.

7

The Talent Show Story

Early in 2012, a five-part series aired on ITV called *The Talent Show Story*. It was a reminder that reality television was not, in fact, a new phenomenon, but harked back decades to the likes of *Opportunity Knocks*, possibly the granddaddy of all talent shows, hosted by the late Hughie Green. The series featured salutary tales such as that of Lena Zavarony, the former child star who died at the age of thirty-five after a lifelong battle with anorexia. Clearly there was a downside to early fame! For obvious reasons, the dominant figure throughout the series was Simon Cowell, who had single-handedly transformed Saturday night television viewing, and many of the stars featured had been created by him. The most obvious example was Susan Boyle, who was interviewed on the first programme, while One Direction featured in the second episode, alongside JLS and Alexandra Burke.

One reviewer of the boys' live shows, Lisa Verrico in *The Times*, made the direct connection between those older reality shows and the fresh new act on the stage today. 'Their short, filler-stuffed show was fun of the old-fashioned, clean-cut variety,' she wrote. 'Outfits included corduroy jackets, braces and V-neck jumpers in sludgy colours. Even trawling through tweets from fans, huddled together on a sofa, One Direction had the aura of an act invented for 1970s teatime TV.' They had brought boy bands back into fashion, she said; it was 'a job decently done'.

Kitty Empire in the *Observer* was similarly complimentary. 'They are undeniably charming with it,' she wrote. 'Opener "Na Na Na" finds 1D at a notional beach, wearing nautical colours, lolloping around like foals loosed in the men's department of H&M. Whoever isn't singing is tasked with whipping up the shrieks. For the benefit of those not au fait with *The X Factor*, there's no official lead singer, but Harry Styles, a phenomenon of tousled hair, is the seventeen-year-old alpha puppy. When he chats to the crowd, the screech goes exponential. This later provides ample cover for a stage-hand trying to steer a prop campfire into position in time for the medley.' She also commented on the fact that, on stage at least, there were no official dance routines. This was unusual for a boy band, but it brought home the fact that all five had originally started as solo acts. It also meant that, post crash and suffering from whiplash, they were still able to go out and perform.

Harry's growing popularity was also commented on by Simon Price in the *Independent on Sunday*. 'Tonight, the boys almost literally step out of a pin-up poster magazine,' he wrote. 'In inane introductory profiles we learn that, for example, Harry likes crispy rolls and girls, and dislikes beetroot. This is greeted with ear-splitting screams from the 99.9 per cent female audience. There is, you see, a One Direction pecking order, and empirical research provides me with the following findings: moptopped Harry Styles is by far the most popular. Close your eyes and guess when Harry's on lead, from the spike in decibels. You'll never be wrong.' Indeed, Harry was indisputably getting the most attention, despite the ongoing controversy about Caroline Flack.

With the crash safely behind them, One Direction had taken to playing pranks on one another when they were asleep on the tour bus. 'The other day Liam was asleep and Zayn shaved a slit in his eyebrow,' Harry told the *Sun*. 'And then Zayn was asleep and I shaved my initials into his leg hair.' It was sometimes easy to forget that in many ways the boys were still ordinary teenagers getting up to jolly japes: with all the touring and the discipline of rehearsing, recording and preparing for the forthcoming onslaught on the United States, they needed some outlet for releasing stress.

As Harry and the crew arrived in London, where the show continued to garner good reviews, the papers were full of older women confessing to taking much younger lovers and talking about how happy it made them feel. 'Harry Styles and his frothy hair get the lion's share of the love,' wrote Caroline Sullivan in the *Guardian*, and she, too, pointed out that they were different from many other boy bands. As well as not dancing, One Direction were, well, rather posher than most boy bands out to make an impression. Their look tended to be a little preppy, heavily reliant on chinos and freshly laundered shirts. Blazers were not unknown. In reality, none of them was actually posh, but it was a look that suited them, not least because it made them stand out from the crowd. 'Screw Bieber fever,' tweeted one fan, 'I've got a One Direction infection.' So, it seemed, had hundreds of thousands of her peers.

Plans to crack the US market continued, with speculation that both Disney and Nickelodeon were interested in getting the boys to appear, which, if it came off, would prove a huge boost to their careers Stateside. Meanwhile, the tour moved to Ireland, where they proved to be as popular as everywhere else: Mullingar native Niall was in his element, introducing the boys to the joys of Irish sausages and generally larking it up.

Despite the workload, they hadn't lost their sense of humour. The Brit Award nominations had been announced, with One Direction featuring in the line-up, and the boys' reaction was to post a spoof video on YouTube of them body-building in preparation for picking up their first Brit award.

This was when Harry and Caroline decided to go their separate ways – in truth, Harry had so much to preoccupy him that it had proved difficult to see one another, not that it took Harry long to find new amours. Caroline, meanwhile, was seen swapping telephone numbers with twenty-one-year-old *The Only Way is Essex* star Joey Essex. Harry was finally beginning to benefit financially from all his success, too, and with some of his spoils he bought a second-hand Range Rover Sport from his stepfather – it didn't go uncommented upon that the insurance alone would have cost him £15,000 a year.

Towards the end of January 2012, One Direction paid a visit to the United States to test the waters, where they were mobbed as they made their way through Hollywood. As scenes flashed back across the Atlantic of hysterical fans attempting to get close to the band, it looked increasingly certain that they were going to make it in America, a notoriously difficult feat.

Harry, as ever, was proving to be the most popular of the five: with his floppy hair, sweet smile, British accent and laid-back charm, he epitomized what American women thought of as the archetypal British male. 'The One Direction boys have been mobbed since arriving in Hollywood, despite not being very well known over here,' one show-business insider told the *Sun*. 'The girls are all going barmy. They love the lads' accents, and Harry's floppy hair is going down a storm. The band have been working on their tans, lying around their swimming pool at the W Hotel in West Hollywood. Stacks of over-excitable female fans have been camped outside the place screaming and generally causing a stir.'

All the papers reported on the amount of attention they were receiving, some from very auspicious quarters indeed: Arnold Schwarzenegger's twenty-two-year-old daughter Katherine tweeted that she thought Harry was a 'cutie'. And she wasn't alone. *Heat* magazine conducted a poll of the 101 Hottest Hunks in the World, and all of One Direction featured in it, with Harry ranking the highest at number eighteen. David Beckham was number one, but it was surely only a matter of time before Harry replaced him.

Harry was rather pleased about Katherine Schwarzenegger, who had tweeted, 'Just watched my first One Direction video with my cousin and @Harry_Styles is a cutie indeed!' 'Katherine's been in the studio watching us,' he told the *Sun*. 'Imagine having Arnie as your dad-in-law. "Leave my house if you want to live."' (Said in an Arnie accent.) He also revealed that life wasn't entirely easy in the public eye – the boys had to use the hotel's service lift as fans would spend the day riding up and down in the guest elevators in the hope of bumping into their idols.

Harry turned eighteen on 1 February 2012, which meant that he was finally allowed to drink in the company of his older lady friends – in the UK, at least. At the same time there were reports that the US management wanted to push him forward as the band's frontman. The band still had no lead singer as such, but it was undeniable that Harry received the lion's share of attention and their management wanted to capitalize on that. The band had filmed a guest slot on *iCarly*, the hit teen television show on Nickelodeon, and it was Harry who had the starring role, with Carly, played by Miranda Cosgrove, developing a crush on him. Harry, however, was wary of shifting the status quo – as were the other boys. The set-up had worked very well for them to date, so why risk upsetting a winning formula? And why risk antagonizing the other band members? They were very much equal members of the band and no one wanted to meddle with that.

The trip to America was a brief one and the boys soon returned to London, meeting Kylie Minogue, no less, in first class. Harry was seen shortly afterwards at a dinner party in trendy East London members' club Shoreditch House, organized by Radio 1 DJ Nick Grimshaw. Harry, now allowed to drink, was seen deep in conversation with Pixie Geldof, but although there was intensive speculation about the exact nature of their relationship, the two were destined to remain just friends. Instead, Harry was seen at west London bar The Social with someone the papers delightedly referred to as a 'mystery blonde', who was clearly in her twenties. (Caroline, meanwhile, was seen kissing twenty-four-year-old Sam McCarthy, from New Zealand band Kids of 88.) Harry's reputation as a ladies' man was growing by the day. Fellow *X Factor* contestant Matt Cardle certainly thought so: 'Harry is going to be fine – the guy hasn't got any problems and not a care in the world,' he said in the wake of Harry's split from Caroline. 'Now he's turned eighteen I think he'll be an absolute nightmare, but then I would be if I was in his position. If we went out on a night together he'd probably snatch up everything in sight. It's a shame they've split as they would have had lovely babies. Caroline is a lovely-looking girl and from what I hear Harry is a pretty-looking boy.'

It seemed the stress of his life was starting to take its toll, though, as Harry had developed a bad back and been told by his management to take up Pilates in order to sort it out as they had a lot more touring ahead of them. 'What Makes You Beautiful' was now topping the charts all over the world, as was their debut album, which went straight in at number one in Italy, Sweden, the Philippines, Hong Kong and Thailand. The boys were a huge hit in Japan and all over the Far East, as well as in Europe and America: they were now a truly global phenomenon.

Meanwhile, Harry's reputation as a ladies' man continued to grow. He was seen at a party thrown by Stella McCartney after her fashion show at Mason's Yard, where he was spotted chatting animatedly to Alexa Chung and the model Poppy Delevingne. The latter, at least, was very impressed: 'I have a total crush on Harry,' she told the *Sun*. 'He walked past me and I was salivating. I like his curly hair.' The two had a bop at the bash, prompting yet more speculation about the nature of their relationship. As Harry complained at one point, every time he was seen with a girl, it was automatically assumed that she was his next girlfriend. There was also gossip about his friendship with Georgia May Jagger, Sir Mick's daughter, which again proved to be false.

In the meantime, the group's next single 'One Thing' had been released as a second offering in various parts of Europe and the third in the UK. Written by Rami Yacoub, Carl Falk and Savan Kotecha, the accompanying video showed the boys larking around in London, performing on the top of a bus, on park steps and in front of a group of buskers. Widely praised for its fresh-faced simplicity, it has gone on to receive 160 million hits on YouTube. The boys thoroughly enjoyed making it: 'It was amazing,' Harry told Capital FM. 'It was literally us being idiots around London for a day and we filmed it.'

The critics were very enthusiastic. *PopMatters*'s Zachary Houle compared 'One Thing' with the Backstreet Boys single 'I Want It That Way': 'The song has a melody that nicks quite liberally from the chorus of the Backstreet Boys' monster hit "I Want It That Way" – so much so that Nick Carter, A. J. McLean and company have a pretty compelling case to launch a plagiarism lawsuit if they really want to. Homage or theft? You decide,' he wrote. Brian Mansfield from *USA Today* also made the comparison: 'Boy-band fans from a previous generation may hear echoes of the Backstreet Boys' "I Want It That Way" in "One Thing". That nod to history may or may not be intentional, but the effect is the same,' he declared. *Entertainment Weekly*'s Adam Markovitz said the song was 'irresistibly bouncy'. Lewis Corner of *Digital Spy* gave the song four out five stars, praising the guitar riff, 'forceful' chorus and catchy melody, and summarizing it as an 'arena-ready hit'. Jason Lipshutz of *Billboard* said the single was 'perfectly executed pop rock', and claimed it 'could own radio for months'.

'What Makes You Beautiful' was still doing pretty well for them, too. It won the 2012 Brit Award for Best Single, although Harry embarrassed himself slightly by thanking Radio 1 in his acceptance speech, when the award was voted for by Capital FM listeners. He made up for it, though, by dedicating the award to the fans: 'Everything we do is for you and this is yours.' Even so, the band was forced to issue an apology as Capital refused to play the song or mention their tour: 'The boys were caught up in the excitement of winning,' they said in a statement. 'The band would like to thank all the Capital Radio listeners for their support and for voting for them.' They didn't brood too long, though – Harry informed the *Daily Express*, 'I'll put it on display in my toilet. You don't want to put it somewhere too show-offy, like in the hall or on your mantelpiece. If you put it in the bathroom everyone's going to have to go in there at some point anyway.'

One Direction then put in a promotional appearance in Paris, where they were mobbed at the Gare du Nord train station and had to rely on their security guards to hold back the fans – this was becoming par for the course by now. Harry in particular was the focus of attention, and he was absolutely mobbed by girls wanting to get close to him at the Sony Belvedere party at the Arts Club. Meanwhile tickets for the March 2013 tour went on sale and sold out so fast that extra dates had to be added. Again, social media was used to bump up interest: 'We are adding more dates and shows as quick as we can! Keep trying guys!' they tweeted, prompting any number of responses from the fans. 'Got my tickets and I'm so happy!' one fan called Laura wrote on the boys' Facebook page. 'I love One D!' another fan, Caitlin Mahon, posted. 'Cannot wait to see those beautiful boys!' said Grace Dallimore, 'Happiest day of my whole entire life.' Fans were camping out on the streets for up to forty hours (many accompanied by parents), using camping equipment for two nights on the pavement. 'My daughter loves One Direction and I'd do anything for her,' said a typical mother, Sam Horrocks, from Castle Bromwich, West Midlands.

At the end of February, the boys returned to North America, or more specifically Canada, where there were further scenes of mass hysteria. Such was the furore that city officials had to close some roads in Toronto, where the boys were making their first appearance on Canadian TV. They were fast turning into as big a sensation there as everywhere else. The show they were appearing on was called *MuchMusic*, and the screaming in the studio was so loud the boys could hardly make themselves heard. Fans threw gifts at the boys, as the barriers struggled to hold them back, and placards and banners were waved. It was pandemonium all over again.

Back in the UK, Harry moved into a new flat: a £575,000 number in trendy east London, complete with its own Japanese zen garden. He also splashed out on a work of art called *If You Remember Me, Then I Do Not Care If Everyone Else Forgets* by Hayden Kays, which was, poignantly, about broken hearts. 'The meaning behind the piece is love and loss. Most of my work is on that theme and it's also to do with a broken heart,' Kays told the *Sun*. 'I love that Mr Styles is digging my vibe. I was a bit surprised when I heard he had bought it. I actually met them all last year at *The X Factor* and he was the nicest of them. He was taking it all in his stride – the others were like rabbits in the headlights.'

Harry wasn't going to have much time to relax though: the forthcoming US tour was taking up everyone's time and energy. A feud was being manufactured by the media between One Direction and The Wanted: the latter's single 'Glad You Came' had entered the charts at number five, while 'What

Makes You Beautiful' was not yet in the Top 10. The Wanted's Max George was happy to stoke the tensions: 'I don't think people look at us over there as the same kind of band because people look at them more like a Jonas Brothers sort of band that are very TV and children's magazine based,' he said. 'They make magazines instead of actually being heard on the radio. We're more of a music band.' It was a dig, but One Direction would have the last laugh as they went on to wow the States, overshadowing The Wanted as they did so.

The tour – ten dates supporting US band Big Time Rush – started in Chicago on 24 February and took in Nashville, Toronto, Detroit and Washington, before ending up in New York. The schedule took its toll. 'I get ill all the time – it's all the travelling and long-distance flights,' Harry told the *Daily Mirror*. 'Four of us had to have vitamin jabs because we were run down. I had mine in my bum. I do get homesick, too.'

The rewards were worth it, though. Girls adored them, following them everywhere and coming up with ever more inventive ways to attract their idols' attention: in Boston, five fans came dressed up as the five band members. Indeed, when they played New York's Radio City Music Hall to a 6,000-strong crowd, prompting yet more comparisons with The Beatles and the Stones, the boys were so overexcited by the occasion that they got too rowdy in a late-night bowling alley after the show and ended up hurling bowling balls so hard they destroyed the machinery. They got a ticking off from the record label, but in many ways it was inevitable: they were young – much younger than The Beatles or the

Stones at a comparable point in their careers – and newly arrived in Manhattan. Of course they were excited; how could they be anything else?

While comparisons with The Wanted continued, the hysteria surrounding One Direction was, if anything, getting worse. An appearance on *The Today Show* drew 15,000 adoring fans; security was beefed up and they were told not to go out in public – when Niall attempted to take pictures of Times Square, he was ordered back to his hotel. Their album *Up All Night* had by now topped the US iTunes chart, prompting yet more comparisons with Beatlemania. The boys were the first to laugh it off, but the interest they generated, and the success they were having, was certainly reminiscent of the Fab Four, even if their music was a little different.

Sonny Takhar, the MD of Syco, told the *Guardian* that at least some of their success was due to the power of social media. 'Sometimes you feel the song's the star, but it's not like that here – it's the act,' he said. 'It's a real moment. Social media has become the new radio; it's never broken an act globally like this before.' But, of course, the act had to be good enough to garner the attention. It might have been a new kind of marketing, but the talent still had to be up to scratch.

The boys were fully aware of how they were being marketed. 'Our tour manager told us it would take three years of hard graft to do well in America . . . so for it to have taken off as it has is incredible,' Liam told the *Daily Mirror*. 'Twitter has been a major factor in getting our name out there in the States. Just as Twitter has gone up, so we have, too. They've gone hand in hand. And, picturewise, Tumblr has helped us a lot. It has really accelerated our success.'

Harry understood the importance of social media, emphasizing that the band took care of their own Twitter feed, rather than employing someone else to do it. 'It's really important that we connect directly with our fans through the likes of Twitter, so they can get to know us,' he told the *Guardian*. 'There would be no point someone in the office doing it because that would defeat the object. We kept in contact with them and gave them something to look forward to.' It was a strategy that was working well.

The success was staggering. In three weeks 'What Makes You Beautiful' had sold more than 260,000 records and was the most requested track on US radio. They became the first ever British pop group to debut at number one on the US album chart, something denied even to the Beatles and the Stones. Harry was as staggered as anyone else: 'For us to even be here and have this kind of reaction is just incredible,' he told the *Daily Mirror*. 'People are being so, so nice and welcomed us so much, and for them to have taken the interest that they have in us feels pretty special. We're not really thinking too far ahead. It's all still sinking in, really.'

Harry still couldn't resist being his exuberant self. When visiting a radio station, he produced a picture of the television reality star Kim Kardashian and scribbled a note for her to call him. Nor could he control his delight at what was happening. 'We'll have a party when we get a chance, but first of all we're definitely going to get Simon Cowell to cough up and take us out for dinner in LA,' he told the *Sun*. 'We're just five normal lads from the UK. What has happened to us is incredible. I know it sounds like a massive cliché, but it's truly amazing – it's what dreams are made of. Just over a year ago we were five boys who didn't know each other. Now we're five best friends having amazing things happen to us. We really are truly grateful to every one of our fans, to anyone who has ever supported us in any way. We just want to thank everyone, everyone is amazing.'

But so were the boys. They had, in an incredibly short space of time, become one of the most successful acts Britain had ever produced, and they were loving every minute of it. From *The X Factor* to touring small-scale venues in Britain to cracking the United States – even their heroes Take That hadn't managed as much. And the band had hardly begun.

8

The British are Coming

The boys had done it. Musical history had been made. They were the first British group in history to have got to number one in America with their debut album, and everyone involved was absolutely ecstatic. Simon Cowell was the first to congratulate them: 'I couldn't be happier for One Direction; it is an incredible achievement,' he said. 'They deserve it. They have the best fans in the world.'

Harry, needless to say, was beside himself. 'It's beyond a dream come true for us,' he said. 'We want to thank each and every one of our fans in the US who bought our album, and we would also like to thank the American public for being so supportive of us.'

Others were similarly unstinting in their praise. Former *X Factor* star Olly Murs called the achievement 'amazing stuff', while a generous Caroline Flack tweeted, 'Incredible news for One D!!!! HUGE news x.' Given the treatment she'd received from some Twitter users in the past, it was pretty magnanimous stuff. It was also confirmed that the boys would be appearing on Nickelodeon, as well as in a further string of cities across the US, such as Fairfax, Virginia; Las Vegas; Los Angeles and New York. It was the best performance by any British band since 1997, when the Spice Girls had entered the US charts at number six with their album *Spice* – but even the mighty Spices hadn't done as well as this.

'It's so surreal,' said Harry. 'We're normal lads, but the Americans can see we're real friends and brothers on stage.' Offstage, it was business as usual, with rumours about Kim Kardashian continuing to circle. Harry's charm was clearly just as effective in the United States as it was back home.

Back in the UK, the comedian David Walliams interviewed Simon Cowell for the *Independent* newspaper, during which Cowell announced that he was most proud of finding One Direction because they hadn't existed before the show. 'At the time there were a couple of people, Harry and Liam, who were really good on their first auditions and we were really disappointed that, for whatever reason, they didn't make the cut on the second round,' he said. 'As they went I said, "I think there's five guys here who we should consider putting into a group," and it literally took ten, fifteen minutes to make that decision. And now this week they've debuted at number one on the American album chart, which is the first time that's ever happened with a British group.'

As for the future, Cowell was sanguine. 'Well, you take it week by week,' he said. 'There's definitely a future for them. They've been signed up by Nickelodeon, they have a movie deal on offer. There's something special about these boys, so

I am proud of that because, and I've got to be honest with you, I'm fifty-two years old and there does come a point when you're on one of these shows and you have to wonder if your opinion is relevant any more.' Cowell's opinion had certainly still been relevant on this one – no one involved could believe the full extent of the boys' success.

One group of people who were less than thrilled were The Wanted, who had done nothing like as well in America as 1D and had been unwise enough to start a war of words with their competitors. They were canny enough to keep schtum on the latest developments, although Tom Parker had commented earlier, and while The Wanted were a few years older than their rivals, One Direction were coming across as the more mature of the two. 'I think it's all pretty silly to be honest,' said Louis to *In:Demand*. 'We are two boy bands, but we actually make quite different music.' It was a point well made, and taken on board by The Wanted, who appeared to regret their earlier remarks. 'When someone takes your words and twists them its like a knife in the back #whathappenedtothegoodguys?!' ran one anguished tweet.

In the meantime, the American fans just couldn't get enough of the One Direction boys. When they appeared at a shopping mall in Natick, Massachusetts, they were mobbed by 5,000 fans. When they were travelling through the streets of Nashville, Tennessee in a limousine, they were chased by 200 girls. Although Harry remained the most popular, the others were also making their mark: at a signing in Long Island, one girl touched Zayn's hand and promptly fainted.

'That was probably the weirdest thing I've ever experienced,' he later recalled.

Some people couldn't help but take a jaundiced view, though. 'This can't be right,' said *Rolling Stone* magazine. 'Didn't the last boy-band era just end?' That said, it also noted the One Direction/The Wanted rivalry, comparing it to a 'Backstreet Boys vs 'N Sync rivalry for the Recession Generation'. Others were more positive. 'They came in at the right time, they let the viral sensation just happen,' said Rachel Chang, editor of teen magazine *J-14*. 'Girls began feeling as if they found them on their own – like they did with Justin Bieber.'

The boys, meanwhile, were preparing to appear at the prestigious Kids' Choice Awards. Not only did Harry continue to be the most popular member of the band with their female fans, but teenage boys were also beginning to copy his look. The resemblance to a young Mick Jagger was becoming even more pronounced.

The Wanted continued to make peace. Siva Kaneswaran was now keen to take a different tack by pointing out that both groups had Irish members. 'We met the One Direction guys when we were performing on *The X Factor* and they were just starting out; they are nice guys,' he said. 'We both have our markets and styles, but there is room for us all. The two big boy bands at the moment have Irish guys in them, so that says it all doesn't it? Listen up, if you want to make it big and if you want to make it in America, you should always have an Irish guy.'

As the boys continued their conquest of the United States,

the downsides of touring became evident. They were still very young and Harry was suffering from homesickness: he had, after all, only recently left home, and he'd always been extremely close to his family. His hobby had been cooking for them, and that was firmly off the agenda at the moment – you could scarcely spend half your time breaking the United States and the rest of it slaving over a hot stove. For all the excitement and new experiences, there was precious little domesticity in his life at the time. In the UK, fans were concerned One Direction would decide to base themselves permanently in the States, but the boys were keen to put it on record that they had no intention of permanently leaving home.

Back in the UK, Caroline Flack was still recovering from all the fuss her relationship with Harry had caused. It was 'really tough' to deal with she told the *Sun*, adding, 'Everyone had an opinion on me and Harry, which was the hardest thing. I learned a difficult lesson. In future, the easiest thing is I keep it to myself.' It was a lesson Harry's future girlfriends would also have to learn.

Rather bizarrely, given that there would be a fair few future girlfriends, rumours were also circulating that Harry and Louis Tomlinson were in a relationship, leading some people to dub them Larry Stylinson (after Brangelina et al). The rumours seemed to have started because the US audiences couldn't understand that the boys' closeness was based on friendship and nothing more, although it has to be said that Harry and Louis did have a tendency to camp it up a little. 'My first crush was Louis Tomlinson,' Harry said in a lighthearted interview. 'It's a mutual feeling. We've discussed it. Louis makes me laugh.' 'Some people genuinely think we're in a relation-ship,' Louis told a Texas radio station. 'I was looking at this thing the other day and they genuinely, seriously think that we're in a relationship. It's so funny!'

He made light of it, but it was absolutely true that some of their fans had got hold of the wrong end of the stick. There were online forums testifying as much: 'Larry Stylinson is basically Louis and Harry's hidden romance that they won't admit to but every Directioner knows is going on,' one fan wrote to another. 'You should watch all of their videos and do a lot of research about them since you're new and haven't been with them since the beginning.' In actual fact, Louis had been with his girlfriend Eleanor Calder for six months now, while behind the scenes Harry was quite the ladies' man.

As the boys continued to make their mark on the United States, The Wanted weren't the only people watching events unfold with interest. Given all the comparisons with Beatle-mania, Sir Paul McCartney felt the need to speak out. 'I hear One Direction are doing really well in America. Good on them – they seem like nice boys. But there are so many bands who get called "the next Beatles". It's the kiss of death,' he warned the boys on ITV1's *Daybreak*. 'Suddenly it puts an awful lot of pressure on them to be the next Beatles. Oasis were "the next Beatles" once. It's a pressure, because suddenly you've got to live up to all the things that we did, and it was a different time. Let's just call them the next terrific band. Doing well in America – good luck lads.'

It was a generous sentiment, although one can't help feeling that there was a little more to it than at first meets the eye. Sir Paul is known for being competitive, and it can't have been easy watching a new generation emerge, threatening to seize the crown, although Sir Paul did follow up his comments by saying he'd be prepared to perform with them. McCartney had caused a stir some years earlier when he'd pointed out that he could write a Beatles song better than Noel Gallagher, and there was a sense that he was happy to have seen that particular competition off. The boys themselves were always the first to distance themselves from any potentially dangerous comparisons, but they were certainly succeeding in a way that almost no other British outfit had done before. The Wanted, meanwhile, once more ventured into contentious territory, with Jay McGuiness announcing, 'We want to become a huge global act and be able to go to every country and sell out a gig. In all honesty, we want to be as big as The Beatles.' Some things are best left unsaid.

One person who took a more measured, and possibly more accurate, view of One Direction's success was DJ Paul Gambaccini, who pointed out that, yes, they were not The Beatles, but that what they had achieved was still extraordinary. '1D have achieved something incredible with their album and the speed of their success,' he wrote in the *Sun*. 'What makes their achievement even more jaw-dropping is that they have got this level of success in America without a huge single under their belts. That is only possible now because of the power of social media [. . .] There was also a gap to fill.

Every generation needs its own fresh pop experience. America was ready for a boy band and they didn't have one of their own. Now they have fallen in love with not one but two British boy bands at once.'

The boys themselves didn't let it faze them. They appeared at the Nickelodeon Kids' Choice Awards in LA, where they met Michelle Obama backstage – Harry made the President's wife laugh when he asked if it was difficult to order pizza from the White House. They performed 'What Makes You Beautiful', triggering such a rapturous response from the audience that they even threatened to overshadow the great Justin Bieber (who, incidentally, was slimed at the event.) Their popularity seemed to grow by the day.

Justin himself had noticed his rivals and was as impressed by them as everyone else was. His attitude to the hoopla they were generating was level-headed, but though still only eighteen himself, he was already a showbiz veteran by this point and knew exactly what they could expect. 'The single guys from One Direction are going to have a lot of fun,' he told the *Daily Mirror*. 'They look great, they sound great and, when you add their British accents into the mix, the American girls are going crazy for them. Sure you need the talent, but you need to win over the American public, that's what it's all about. One Direction are genuine good guys. The industry needs a fresh boy band, and by the end of this year they will be the biggest boy band in the world.' He went on to hint darkly that he knew of a megastar who had a crush on Harry, but he refused point blank to be drawn into revealing who it was. If it was Taylor Swift he wasn't saying, even though that particular relationship was still some way off.

'What Makes You Beautiful' was finally released in the States in April and promptly soared up the charts. Reports surfaced that the boys had been told to avoid having girl-friends in order not to discourage the fans while they were in such demand, but in fact, nothing could have been further from the truth. Harry, in particular, had been enjoying himself. Once One Direction left the States for Australia, it emerged that he had been seeing another older woman, twenty-four-year-old Sarah-Louise Colivet, a photographer from Kildare. Her mother Jacinta was actually the one to spill the beans: 'It's true, she has struck up a friendship with him. She rang and said he was lovely, great fun and a really nice guy,' she said. 'She met him in New York – she is a cool customer though so she wasn't going to tell her mum too much. I don't think she realized that girls go that crazy for him until now. He has gone on to Australia now, but they will definitely stay in touch.' The two had met after a One Direction gig, but it wasn't to last in the longer term – Harry was simply too busy, too much in demand and the timing wasn't right. Sarah-Louise was fortunate, though, as she received nothing like the kind of abuse Caroline had had to put up with; she was even on the receiving end of some praise, from people who told her she was pretty and deserved Harry. Sensibly, Sarah-Louise kept her head down and said nothing.

Even so, it escaped no one's notice that she was twenty-four. This time round it was a six-year age difference rather than fifteen and, at eighteen, Harry had edged a little closer to manhood, but even so, it was becoming clear that his relationship with Caroline Flack wasn't a one-off: Harry had a marked taste for older women.

There were reports that Harry had been dating US singer Lily Halpern, but they were wide of the mark. What was more interesting to 1D fans, although it would take some time to develop into anything, was when it emerged that Taylor Swift was the major star with a crush on Harry. The two had met at the Nickelodeon awards, and Taylor – another older woman, although at twenty-two the age gap was narrowing – had been very impressed. 'Taylor is a huge One Direction fan and was excitedly bopping along to the boys when they performed on stage,' a witness who had been backstage at the time told the *Daily Mirror*. 'Then she was chatting to Justin and told him how hot she found Harry. Justin was joking about trying to keep his own girlfriend, Selena Gomez, away from the band because she, too, loves them. Taylor went backstage and was hanging around by the group's dressing room, and said a quick "hello" to the guys. She started dramatically fanning herself afterwards, making out like she was overwhelmed, which got everyone laughing. She really likes Harry, but made Justin promise not to go on the record about it.'

As it happened, Harry had been pretty impressed himself. 'I feel good,' he said. 'I think the people who were getting involved are all great performers, so for them to enjoy our performance was nice. Katy Perry was there and Selena

Gomez. There was Ashley Tisdale. Taylor Swift was dancing as well . . .' He didn't say any more at the time, but Taylor had obviously made an impression. It was just that Harry had a few more wild oats to sow first.

He also expressed an interest in reality television star Jillian Harris, who is fourteen years his senior. Evidently not short of confidence, Harry spotted her in a restaurant at the W Hotel, sauntered across and asked for her telephone number. For once, the famous Styles charm didn't work. 'I am way too old for you,' was Jillian's answer to her young admirer, as she later told the *Sunday Mirror*. 'He asked for my phone number. He looked cute and adorable, but he was also very young looking. I am sorry but I could never date an eighteen-year-old. I don't think that's even legal in the US, is it? We were seated just behind Harry's table. I didn't even know who Harry was. I listen to country music and I had never heard of One Direction, but my friend did and pointed him out to me.

'When we got up to leave, he walked straight up to me and said he would like to take me out for dinner. I didn't know what to say. I think I just laughed. Then he said he was playing a concert in Canada later this year. I told him that maybe my friend and I would come to the show. He said he would like that, then he asked for my phone number. I can't remember what I said. I don't think I was rude. I just laughed and told him I was way too old for him. He didn't seem too put out. He was very sure of himself actually. Harry is cute and if I was twenty-one, I would be all over him. But I'm thirty-two and I just don't think that would be appropriate.' It wasn't a reaction Harry got very often.

The only small fly in the ointment was One Direction itself – or to be more accurate, an American boy band called One Direction that had nothing to do with their UK counterpart. They and their manager, Dan O'Leary, who was the father of the group's lead singer, Sean, had been watching in slack-jawed fury as the UK's One Direction cleaned up: they'd had nothing like the same success and were furious at what they saw as the appropriation of their name. They decided to launch a lawsuit against Simon Cowell and the boys, incurring the fury of fans of the UK One Direction in the process.

Alleging that they had been using the name since 2009, they sued for $1 million and three times the profits the UK band had made. 'He's mad if he thinks we're going to lie down, sit down or back down over this,' said Dan of Simon Cowell. 'We're not going to be pushed around by some music mogul. The British One Direction have Mr Cowell's enormous resources behind them. We, on the other hand, do not. In our view, we were here first. We have rights, we have talent and we have heart. My boy's dreams and the dreams of the band are just as important as the dreams of Cowell's group.'

That might have been so, but he was right: he didn't have Cowell's power or clout. And anyway, by this time the British One Direction had well and truly established themselves, so why on earth should they give up their name? It was a pressure they could have done without, but the boys had no option but to shrug it off and get on with the job. Their fans were not so sanguine, however, and started issuing hate mail and death threats, particularly to Dan O'Leary, who was seen as the instigator of the action. Sean talked about the death threats his father had received, but given the strength of feeling the fans had displayed in the past, it shouldn't have been that big a surprise.

By this time the boys were in Australia, where they were proving just as popular as they had in the States. Coincidentally, the singer Rihanna was in Australia at the same time and let it be known that she, too, found Harry quite cute; she thought he had star quality, and Harry was clearly delighted. 'That is absolutely incredible,' he said. 'I'd love to hook up.' In truth, everyone was playing it up a little – Rihanna and Harry? Well, of course not, but it made good copy while it lasted.

The boys continued to enjoy themselves in their spare time; they were pictured splashing about on Sydney's Manly beach, while speculation intensified as to who Harry would go for next. By now, Harry was allowed to go out drinking, which he did one night with Zayn. They went to the Scary Canary bar and ended up judging a wet T-shirt competition of all things. Backpacker Emma Carrigan witnessed the whole thing: 'It was crazy, we go there every night and it has never been as mobbed as it was when the two of them walked in,' she told the *Daily Mirror*. 'They had been to the Ivy in George Street and Harry told us it was too quiet and boring for them in there and he wanted to go somewhere more lively. The crowd were bombarding the boys and throwing themselves at them.

It was so bad that one of their bouncers had to ask for an area to be cordoned off. Zayn picked out ten girls from the crowd to join them, but he was the quieter of the two. When a wet T-shirt competition began, Zayn was just looking on and smiling, but Harry went crazy and kept shouting, "Come on, come on!" They were just lovely guys having fun.'

Harry's combination of exuberance and charm was proving utterly irresistible, and both in person and through his public persona he simply couldn't help winning round hearts and minds. Sometimes Harry has a puppyish quality about him, while at other times it's more Jaggeresque – either way, women love him, and so did the male fans, even if they didn't always admit it. Harry was turning into the most fortunate of creatures: the girls wanted to be *with* him and the boys wanted to *be* him. His infectious enthusiasm, combined with his sheer exuberant joy at what was happening to him, was enormously appealing. All of the boys were on a roll, but none more so than Harry.

The dark side of fame was always present, though. When the boys turned up to Sydney's Nova radio station, they all made a great fuss of the receptionist, Anna Crotti, with Harry commenting, 'She's lovely. She's got beautiful eyes and lovely manners.' Zayn then asked her to meet them all for a drink, but when news got out, the trolls appeared in a trice, posting unpleasant messages on Facebook, and phoning the radio station with threats. Anna – who was in a relationship anyway – called off the drink.

9

One Directioners

'There was simply no way this group could fail,' wrote Brisbane-based Lars Brandle on *Billboard.com* when reviewing one of the boys' sell-out Australian shows. 'Hysteria has followed them since they arrived in the country, and this concert served as a mass outpouring of delirium. The crowd, almost entirely comprised of teenage girls, was absolutely wired, fanatical. From the opening support act, the 5,000-plus capacity room created a noise so fierce, it would've drowned out most machines the industrial age came up with . . . For eighty minutes, the young pop stars sang and twirled, and winked at their love-struck fans in the best seats. It was all slick, clean fun, the audience, a colorful caldron of glowsticks and white One Direction T-shirts, lapped it all up.'

This was typical of what was being written about One Direction everywhere they went. Critically and commercially the tour was proving to be a massive success, although there had never been the slightest doubt they would succeed on the latter front. All their concerts sold out within minutes of the details being announced, and many privately considered the venues too small. It was better to err on the side of caution, perhaps, because a half-full stadium would have dented the band's growing reputation, but the fact is that by this time, they would have sold out a huge stadium. The boys were truly a phenomenon. They continued to get mobbed everywhere they went, made headlines simply by putting in an appearance at a new town, and continued to be a security nightmare, albeit through no fault of their own, because they couldn't move without attracting a huge crowd. It was the same everywhere they went: the level of hysteria and attention they provoked certainly set them apart.

As the boys' fame increased, public interest extended to the band members' families as well. And just as Harry had become the best known member of the band, so his mother, Anne, became the most high-profile relative of the band, not least due to her Twitter account, which she kept up regularly, using her new higher profile to raise sponsorship for a charity climb up Mount Kilimanjaro. She was proving extremely popular amongst the fans: Harry ensured that #happybirthdayanne trended on Twitter, while some of the fans had set up pages on Facebook, thanking her for bringing Harry into the world and telling her how good looking she is. They weren't the only ones to think so: Harry's band members had all commented on what an attractive woman she is – much to Harry's embarrassment – while the TV personality Alan Carr called her gorgeous. Anne, like so many of the women associated with Harry, had to put up with a certain amount of online abuse, but she couldn't have handled it better: 'I hope you find inner peace,' she would calmly reply to any unkind comments.

Anne was, of course, overwhelmed by what was happening to her famous son. 'I fill up every time Harry's on TV,' she told the *Daily Mirror*. 'I feel incredibly proud and it's so surreal to see my boy on stage. At the end of the day he's my little baby and he is on stage in front of millions of people.' Millions of adoring people, she could have added. The fans were more devoted than ever, referring to themselves as One Directioners, to their heroes as 1D, and following every move the boys made. The band really had gone global now, wowing everyone they met. About the only person who seemed untouched by the phenomenon was Madonna, who uncharacteristically proved herself out of touch when asked about the band on ITV1's *Daybreak*: 'That's a pop group, right? Sorry.' When she was told they were indeed a pop group, she continued, 'I haven't seen them yet, no, sorry. Slap my hand.' For pop's great survivor not to have heard of the new sensation sweeping the planet was a rare slip indeed.

The boys continued to enchant in Australia, where they were pictured hugging koala bears, before making their way to New Zealand. There, Harry was rumoured to have hooked up with American model Emma Ostilly, after they were seen together at the trendy Gypsy Tea Rooms bar. Harry fuelled the rumours by posting a picture of himself and Emma online, and while it wouldn't lead to a long-term relationship, it did nothing to dispel Harry's growing reputation as a ladies' man. It did, however, lead to the usual problems with trolls, and Emma was forced to delete her Twitter account and change her name on Facebook. Amidst all this partying, the boys managed to fit in a few concerts, too, performing in Auckland and Wellington as they continued their quest for global domination.

In late April, after a hugely successful stint in the United States, Australia and New Zealand, One Direction returned to the UK, where there was talk of them taking a break after their arduous tour. In all honesty, though, everyone was determined to keep the momentum going – a fortnight off was going to be the most they would manage. With Harry's reputation for liking more mature ladies, he couldn't resist telling the *Sun* who his choice of the world's sex symbols would be: Angelina Jolie, Kate Moss and Kate Winslet topped the list. 'I'm not really a pick-up-line guy – I don't know what I do,' he added, somewhat disingenuously. All he had to do was be himself – his natural charm ensured his success.

It continued to cause problems for the women he was associated with, though. When Harry went back to Cheshire to see his family he was pictured with an old friend, Ellis Calcutt: he took her for a spin in his latest car, an Audi R8 coupé, and then on for a coffee. Assuming she was his latest girlfriend, it didn't take long for Twitter to light up with the usual abuse. Ellis decided to grab the bull by the horns and explain the reality of the situation on Facebook, not least the fact that she already had a boyfriend.

'Wow, you people are sooo quick to make up rumours! Me & Harry went for coffee together as we haven't seen each other since last year!' she said. 'We're only good friends and have been since high school. I have a lovely boyfriend called Phil, so you can stop spreading rumours about me and Harry dating each other because we absolutely are not!' Something similar happened to Emma Horan, Niall's cousin. She posted a picture of the two of them on Twitter and immediately got trolled, forcing her to clarify the fact that they were cousins, not romantically linked, and that the other girls mentioned were childhood friends.

Ellis wasn't the only one having to put up with unwanted attention: Harry's family's address had got out and fans had taken to camping around the house. Both Harry's family and the neighbours were a little taken aback, but Harry was a world-famous star now, and a sex symbol to boot. He had accumulated an enormous following and this is what people in his position have to expect. Even so, it was causing a problem for the neighbours, so the family temporarily abandoned their home in Holmes Chapel until Harry went back down south.

It was at about this time that a rite of passage of sorts appeared to take place. Nicky Byrne of the soon-to-be disbanded Westlife seemed to symbolically hand on the boy-band crown, in particular saying that he was pleased Mullingar singer Niall Horan and Dublin's Siva Kaneswaran were enjoying the same kind of success as Westlife. 'I suppose a little bit of me probably thinks I wish I was twenty to do it all over again,' he said rather wistfully. 'But you have to hold your hands up – we've had a wonderful time and it's time to pass the reins on to someone else. You've got The

Wanted coming through and One Direction, and it's brilliant for them. I've met the guys, both bands, lovely guys, an Irish guy in each band, which is great.'

Generous words, and now it was time to plan the next move. It's well known that a band's second album is a lot more difficult to produce than the first, for any number of reasons. Firstly, for bands that come together in a more conventional way, it's often the case that all the songs on the album have been boiling up in the songwriter's head for years, ready to burst out fresh and new for their debut album. To do it all again a year or so later is not so easy, because the ideas that went into the first album had often been forming for a long time. That wasn't quite the case with One Direction, but even so, it was a challenge to find material that was as promising as the tracks that appeared on the first album.

Secondly, of course, there was the weight of expectation. Just as they had found with their second single, people now had something to compare the band to – namely, their own past performance. They had gone straight to the top, a difficult enough feat in itself, but now they had to go one better and stay there. If One Direction slipped up with their second album, they might turn out to be a flash in the pan, but everyone was planning on more than that. Some reality stars went on to find lasting careers – just look at Susan Boyle – and, properly managed, that could be on the cards for One Direction.

It was certainly in everyone's interests to get it right. A great deal of money was at stake, along with quite a few livelihoods, as Nick Gatfield, chairman of Sony Music UK, made clear. 'What you might not know about One Direction is that they already represent a $50 million business,' he told *Music Week*. 'And that's a figure we expect to double next year. The team around them – which includes musicians, stylists, producers, tour managers and so on – accounts for around ninety people. That's ninety jobs created by these five boys.'

So, no pressure, then. The boys themselves certainly realized what was at stake. 'We're trying to get it [the second album] done,' Niall told Ryan Seacrest. 'We're working on it at the moment – recording whenever we can and writing songs on the road. Hopefully, we can get it done by Christmas.' The record company was certainly keen to see the band press ahead, and they paid for the boys to take a trip to Sweden to talk to writers and producers and start recording.

With such huge concerns in the background, it was sometimes a relief to concentrate on the lighter things in life. Harry had always been known for being surprisingly domesticated, as he explained in an interview with the *Daily Star*. 'I've loved cleaning since I was little. I find it very relaxing and calming. I even watch all the TV shows about it to help me with ideas and stuff. I know it sounds weird and the rest of the lads tease me about it, but I just really enjoy cleaning – what can I say? If I ever got messy I know my mum would kill me. I'm happy to help out with anything, whether it's taking bins out, cleaning the kitchens or the bathroom. I make a mean carbonara. People are always complimenting me on my cooking. It must be something people wouldn't think I would be good at but I'm really into it.'

It was an unusual combination: globally famous pop star and ladies' man who also liked to have a good clean-up at home before cooking supper, but then, Harry has a very strong personality and carries it off with panache. Increasingly, there was speculation that Harry might be tempted to go it alone without his band mates: there were rumours that he had been approached by some big corporate names to do ads for them on a solo basis, but it would have been a very high-risk strategy at that stage. Robbie Williams might have launched a hugely successful solo career post-Take That, but Geri Halliwell didn't fare so well after leaving the Spice Girls. It was still very early days if One Direction was aiming for a long-term career as a group, and to risk alienating the others by doing something that would make him stand out on his own didn't make sense. Besides, being in a band helps to deflect at least some of the pressure. The burden falls on five pairs of shoulders, not one, and the same goes for the shared experience. Matters were working out just fine as they were.

Most successful entertainers feel they have to give something back and One Direction is no exception. In May they made the time to meet eight-year-old Niamh Power, who had a brain tumour. She burst into tears of happiness when the charity Rays of Sunshine arranged for the boys to walk into her hotel room in London's Millennium Hotel, posing for pictures with all of them, and was especially delighted when she got a hug and a kiss from Harry. 'She says she's never going to wash that cheek again,' said her mother Marie.

Apart from good works and his career, Harry's love-life was still the source of intense speculation. There were rumours that he was dating twenty-two-year-old Emily Atack, who plays Charlotte Hinchcliffe in *The Inbetweeners*, rumours that were fuelled by a tweet she'd made two years earlier: 'Does Harry from One Direction HAVE to be six-teen?! Let's pretend he's eighteen at least! Then there would only be One Direction he would be going . . . to the bed-room!' Friends said that Harry had a crush on her, too, but there were problems. One Direction were beginning to pre-pare for another major world tour – this time with bigger venues – while Emily was trying to break into films.

Even so, friends briefly hoped the fling would turn into something more. 'They're perfect for each other, they really are,' one of Harry's confidantes told the *Sunday Mirror*. 'They've been getting to know each other and keeping things quiet, but they're close. Harry has always had a crush on her and hoped he could get it together with her and they eventu-ally did.'

Not for long, though, as the timing was definitely not right. Towards the end of May, the boys flew back to the States just as it was announced that 'What Makes You Beautiful' had sold over two million digital copies in the US, yet another milestone achievement of which they could be proud. It was Louis who let slip to the *Daily Mirror* that Harry was back on the market. Asked if he was still dating Emily, Louis replied, 'No, no . . .' Asked who'd had the most luck with girls on the recent tour of the States and Australasia, he replied, 'Do I even need to say who? I think it would be completely unfair to single out girls in that way, or to put it like that. But if you were to put it like that, I think it would – possibly – be . . . Harry. Do we keep a tally? No we do not! That would be hideous.'

Despite the fact that One Direction had been pretty good about rising above their feud with The Wanted, Louis couldn't resist having a little pop. 'I think it is always blown up out of proportion, the way that just because we're two boy bands there's massive rivalry,' he said. 'But we are hoping that they'll still get on with us. Because, you know, there is potentially a spot on our arena tour for them to support us. I was going to say something rude, then. Or something sexual. But that's something The Wanted would say.' You couldn't blame him as The Wanted had rather set themselves up.

There were concerns from some people in the music industry that One Direction were being worked too hard in a bid to capitalize on their success: 'I've never known a band announce a second summer tour before a first summer tour is over. It's insane – they're working them like dogs and print-ing money right now,' said Andy Greene, associate editor of *Rolling Stone* magazine.

But the band members, as much as anyone else, wanted to capitalize on what they had built so far, on top of which, the boys were still young and had an awful lot of energy. The 2013 world tour had been announced: many of the ninety-four gigs had already sold out and a further twenty-five performances were added in twenty US cities. The prices were also going up, with some tickets costing as much as £200: this really was putting them in the same league as the Rolling Stones. There were also special appearances and recording sessions, and the boys had signed a number of endorsement deals with companies like Pokémon, Nokia, HarperCollins and Hasbro. They were taking it all in their stride.

The only real problems came when the fans got overenthusiastic. When they were in New York, Liam and Niall went out on a rare day off with just one member of security: they were instantly mobbed by a crowd of sixty girls who were waiting outside, and the situation quickly turned nasty. Liam was pushed over, while someone accidentally hit Niall in the face; then Liam's shirt was ripped, while clumps of Niall's hair were pulled out. Security tried their best to protect the boys, with the police getting involved, but footage taken by those present showed the situation was totally out of control. The police and security were begging the girls to back off, but they wouldn't: 'I'm not leaving! I feel really bad doing this but I love you Niall!'

On the whole, the boys realized how fortunate they were, always spoke well of the fans and practically never complained about anything, but this was too much. Both boys took to Twitter: 'That wasn't even funny,' snapped Liam. Niall felt the same: 'This is a complete joke,' he tweeted. 'Ridic. Day off. Wanna chill.' A situation like that could have turned extremely dangerous; both boys were shaken and upset and the band was forced, yet again, to beef up their security.

Harry wasn't actually present when it happened, but he knew as well as any of them that their lives had changed and they weren't going to be quite as free as they had been in the past. They were, however, well aware of the fact that they were being given the kind of opportunities most people couldn't even dream of. They would simply have to accept that more security was needed and not go out alone.

Harry remained his cheery self, doing an interview with Radio 1's Nick Grimshaw, in which he happily branched out into the surreal: 'I want to shave my hair off. And I wear crotchless tights,' he began. 'Everyone's telling me not to do it. I think my popularity's in my face and not my hair. I think it would be fine. I was reading a magazine and it was talking about men wearing tights. Basically, it just feels really comfortable, so I've been putting them on under my jeans. So I'm just wondering if you could get me some good ones. Like, some crotchless ones. Just because I've been stealing my sister's. The thing is, I'm not sure if I'm ready to bring them out. Maybe I should just keep them under my trousers for a bit. Do you think they do, like, gold ones?'

He was being silly, but they all needed the release. They joked happily about making a film of *Romeo and Juliet*, with Niall playing the part of Juliet – Niall said he'd be prepared to do it for the good of the group – while there were serious considerations about the boys starring in a film, as, of course, The Beatles had done several times over and several decades earlier. Filming started on a documentary, as well as a 3D concert movie. There was even talk of a cartoon. Meanwhile, their music DVD, *Up All Night: The Live Tour*, had sold 76,000 copies, the first act to outsell the number one US album with a music DVD.

Another downside of fame is that the past has a habit of coming back to haunt you: all the boys had been embarrassed by long forgotten photos that had come to light on sites like Bebo and MySpace. Niall and Louis – who posed topless for various shots – were the most embarrassed, while the others passed it off as youthful larks.

By this stage it was becoming apparent that it wasn't just young girls who were interested in the boys. One Direction had spoken rather wistfully about how much they'd like to have more male fans, but in actual fact it was the mums they had to watch out for, perhaps made hopeful by Harry's fling with Caroline. 'The fans can sometimes get very graphic, and there are a few mums that hit on us,' he said to the *Daily Star*. 'Ask Harry – they just go for it,' added Louis. 'They just grab and pinch and sometimes it gets a bit tricky.'

As a matter of fact, attention was about to shift back to Harry's love-life again, and yet again for all the wrong reasons. It emerged that Caroline Flack was by no means the only older lady to have engaged his attention, and the next name to surface would prove even more controversial than the last. It seemed he just couldn't help it – Harry liked older women, and older women liked Harry – and his good looks and easy charm just kept on bowling them over, one by one.

Attention was temporarily diverted by someone quite different: Justin Bieber. Far from seeing his UK counterparts as a threat, the Canadian heart-throb had always got on very well with, and spoken warmly of, One Direction. Now it looked like they might link up and work together. It would be a marketing man's dream.

'The One Direction guys are great,' he told the *Daily Mirror*. 'We have a lot of fun whenever we hang out. They came over to my house and we were just chilling out around the pool and listening to music. We were talking about me collaborating with them on a song on their next album. It's gonna be great. And I asked them who else they would like to work with. They were, like, Rihanna, Katy Perry, Taylor Swift and Jennifer Lopez. Now don't get me wrong, those are all very talented artists, but there seems to be a pattern emerging and, looking at the smile on the guys' faces, I don't think it was all about the music . . .'

He was right there. Justin – who's not exactly un-sought-after himself – knew very well what it was like to be in the eye of the storm when it came to female attention. 'They sure have an eye for the ladies but, even better for the guys, the ladies have a bit of an eye for them, too,' he said. 'From what I hear they shouldn't have much trouble trying to persuade Rihanna, Katy or Taylor to work with them . . . if you know what I'm saying. The great thing about them is that they might be the biggest band in the world but they have stayed regular guys who are just fun to hang with. I don't see them changing. They are just so grounded and they have each other.' It was a sweet tribute. Justin, of course, had had to cope with fame all on his own.

The boys were going from strength to strength – even if Harry had yet more shocking news to come about his love-life. It only seemed to enhance his reputation and increase interest in the whole band, while making it clear that Harry was his generation's leading ladies' man.

10

Risky Business

The scene was the Manchester radio station Key 103 in August 2011. One Direction had already become famous, but it was still fairly early days: they were promoting their debut single 'What Makes You Beautiful' on the show *In: Demand*, and the DJ was Lucy Horobin. Lucy was thirty-two at the time, Harry was seventeen, and the on-air chemistry between them was undeniable. 'I'm joined by five very handsome and lovely boys and I've got you all to myself tonight,' Lucy began.

'You look lovely today,' said Harry.

'Thanks, Harry, so do you,' Lucy replied.

And so the banter continued. Harry and the boys told Lucy that she would be moving in with them: 'You can cook for us,' said Harry.

Lucy agreed.

'What a woman,' said Harry.

It was Niall's eighteenth birthday, and Lucy gave him a cake, poppers and musical horns. 'Harry, put your horn away,' she added.

'Wow! I like it,' said Harry. 'I love *In: Demand*. I love

In:Demand.' They went on to sing 'What Makes You Beauti-ful', during which Harry was seen gazing intently at Lucy as he mouthed the words, 'I love you.' Shortly after this encoun-ter, they were seen at a Manchester hotel together. Harry had done it again.

In actual fact, that wasn't the first time they'd met – there had been an on-air encounter a month earlier, after which they'd stayed in touch via Twitter and Facebook. This was before Harry met Caroline Flack and before his reputation for having a taste for older women emerged. But there was one big problem here considerably worse than the age differ-ence: Lucy was married. She had tied the knot a year earlier, but she and her husband, Oliver Pope, were going through a rough patch and had entered a separation of sorts, although they were still living in the same house. It's also unclear whether or not Harry knew Lucy was married, but when details of the fling emerged a year later, there was uproar. Yet another older woman and this one with a husband in the background. What next?

The two of them had undeniably hit it off. 'Lucy was right up his street, exactly the type of girl, or woman should I say, he is attracted to,' a friend of Harry's told the *Sunday Mirror*. 'She is sexy, confident and is doing well in her career. But he never wanted anything serious. He's far too young to settle down, and when he met Lucy the band was just beginning to take off massively. He knew she didn't want anything serious either, he thought it a bit of harmless fun.'

Harmless, maybe, were it not for the fact that she had a

husband. Lucy knew her other half would be less than thrilled with the news and was keen to play it down, but a friend revealed that although she, too, saw it as just a fling, Lucy was momentarily very taken with Harry. 'She knows she shouldn't admit it, but she said the sex was amazing,' a friend of Lucy's told the *Sunday Mirror*. 'He knew exactly what he was doing, despite the fact he was only seventeen. He's adorable and Lucy had a lot of fun, but it was never going to be anything serious. It was a mistake. She loves her husband and wants to be with him. She's a great girl but got caught up in the moment with Harry. She was having a few difficulties in her marriage and it just happened. She knows people will hate her for doing it, particularly with a young lad who is so high profile, but life is not always black and white. We all make errors but have to learn from them.'

It was a pretty public lesson, but then so was everything that involved Harry these days. The fling actually went on for a full three months and only ended when Harry met Caroline. When it became public, inevitably the trolls came out in force, insulting and abusing Lucy, just as they did with all Harry's women. Lucy was as taken aback as all the other victims; she confined herself to tweeting an unhappy face, but the furore raged on. Lucy didn't turn up for work the following day – she was by now at Heart South Coast FM – and co-presenter Jason King explained, not altogether tactfully, why she wasn't there. 'Over the weekend you may have picked something up in the newsagents and read something which may have shocked you,' he said. 'I'd like to confirm the rumours are true and she has taken time off – to read *Fifty Shades of Grey* and tell us all about it tomorrow.'

All of this may or may not have provoked Harry into some slightly outrageous behaviour at a concert in Houston, Texas, when he and Niall leaned into one another, looking for all the world as if they were about to share a kiss – they didn't – although it was far too late to deflect attention from the fact that Harry was really more into the ladies. Whatever the case, he was totally unrepentant. Asked by the *Daily Star* if there was an upper age limit for his prospective lady friends, he replied, 'Anything up to my mum's age; she's forty-four!'

He was also keen to spill the beans about past dates. 'I told someone I was gay once. And I went out with a girl who was so shy she barely said a word. I'd say, "What have you been up to?" She'd say, "Not much." She just killed the conversation.' And of his worst kiss: 'Someone cut my lip once. She came in a bit fast, hit my lip onto my tooth and it started bleeding. There was blood everywhere.'

The fans didn't seem to mind too much, hurling their knickers at Harry and the others with abandon, harking back to the heyday of another great sex symbol, Tom Jones. Rather more dangerously, they also started throwing iPhones and keys, seemingly oblivious to the fact that they could do their heroes an injury. Harry's friends couldn't help teasing him about it, too. 'Justin has become really good buddies with the guys, and we know some beautiful young women in the industry who have major crushes on Harry,' said Selena Gomez, Justin Bieber's girlfriend, talking to the *Daily Mirror*.

'He could probably pretty much take his pick from the hottest young girls in Hollywood. But from what Justin has been telling me, it's not the young girls he's looking at. I guess you just can't blame him when you see how hot women such as Cameron Diaz, Eva Longoria, and Sofia Vergara look. Both me and Justin still have really hot mums, and Justin was like, "Harry might have become one of my best buddies, but with his record we need to keep him away from our mums."'

Lucy, meanwhile, had been forced to shut down her Twitter account – something she had in common with a lot of the women Harry had dated – while her husband Oliver clearly felt it was time to give his side of the story. Lucy had already confessed to him, so it hadn't come as a shock, but nor was he exactly thrilled by it all. A friend of Oliver's related it all to the *Sunday Mirror*: 'Oliver was devastated,' he said. 'He told me he said, "Harry Styles? The little scumbag with Caroline Flack?" She nodded and admitted it happened . . . twice. He didn't know how to respond. He was speechless.' Oliver continued, '"I was outraged. The pain was unimaginable. Not only was my wife telling me she had slept with somebody else, she was telling me it was with him – Harry Styles. I was devastated. I felt every emotion . . . hatred, sadness, disappointment. Harry is a predator. Since his fling with Lucy has been revealed, he's been hailed a hero – an innocent lad who just happens to like older women. Teenage boys look up to him. Teenage girls want to be with him."'

'To Oliver, Harry is just a spoilt little rich kid who does whatever he wants, when he wants – no matter the consequences. Just because Harry is young doesn't mean he is some innocent victim being hunted down by older women. In his eyes, it's the women who need to be careful. And men need to be on their guard. It was Harry who asked for Lucy's number. She was feeling low about the state of her marriage – it seemed a bit of fun. He pursued Lucy. It was him who did a lot of the running, sending flirty texts and messages on Twitter. Eventually, after all the flirting they ended up at a hotel. It was the talk of the radio station. Initially Oliver blamed Lucy. Who wouldn't? He threatened to walk away from the marriage. But that was only an option until he calmed down. Lucy refused to give up on their marriage too. At first Ollie found it hard to forgive but he was taken aback by her despair.'

Lucy and Oliver's marriage seemed to have survived, and they appeared to have come through it stronger than ever, but it did make the point that Harry wasn't quite as innocent as he looked.

Not to be outdone, the *Sunday Mirror*'s sister paper found another friend who related how Lucy had told Oliver about Harry. 'Oliver remembers clear as day the moment Lucy sat him down and told him what had happened,' he said. 'They were at home in Manchester but were practically living separate lives. They'd hit a stumbling block in their marriage and that's why Lucy succumbed to the charms of Harry. When she realized what she really wanted, she told Oliver what had happened. She didn't go into every cough and spit of the relationship but pretty much told him everything he needed to know. It was heartbreaking.'

The confession took place in November 2011, when Harry was seeing Caroline, but Oliver found it difficult to deal with initially. 'When Oliver first found out about the fling he couldn't bear to watch TV in case Harry was on it,' said the friend. 'He couldn't bring himself to listen to the radio in case he heard Harry's voice. And he certainly didn't want to open a newspaper in case he saw Harry's face. At the time it was very difficult. One Direction were everywhere.' It seemed to be an episode everyone involved clearly wanted to forget.

Harry himself was keeping a low profile. He was still in the States with the rest of the band; by this time they were in Fort Lauderdale, where the band were performing, and had wisely chosen not to comment. When the band returned to the UK shortly afterwards, some fairly predictable 'Lock up your mothers' headlines appeared, and opinions were split as to who had been most at fault. All things considered, Harry got off pretty lightly and so far hadn't been branded a marriage-wrecker. The man himself, meanwhile, was spotted in the company of an estate agent, checking out properties in London's exclusive Primrose Hill. Harry was earning a lot of money now and clearly wanted to put it to good use.

He was also rumoured to be seeing a new woman: *Made in Chelsea* star Caggie Dunlop, a twenty-three-year-old sex columnist for a national newspaper. The two were seen leaving a nightclub together, although in reality it was nothing particularly serious; at the same time his band mates voiced the increasingly unlikely prediction that Harry would end up alone. 'Harry is the magic match-up man,' said Liam.

'When I got with my girlfriend, Harry was the boy who set us up. And with Louis Tomlinson and Eleanor Calder, it was also Harry. He is like Hitch – he can do for everyone else but not himself. He will end up a lonely old man.'

As if. Harry's charm was such that it worked across the age ranges, and given how many alluring older women were happy to admit to having a crush on him, Harry didn't have to spend so much as a minute alone if he so wished. All the boys were mobbed wherever they went, especially Harry, and this bout of recent revelations had done nothing to dent his popularity. If anything, it had enhanced it by branding him something of a bad boy. It was always the women who got the blame, never Harry – except in the case of an angry husband – and as such he was more desirable than ever. It wasn't as if he was emulating the behaviour of pop stars several decades earlier, who had gone for girls that were much too young: Harry's girlfriends were all well past the age of consent. It didn't do him any harm with the older generation, either – more mature ladies were delighted that a handsome young boy like Harry was interested in them. Not that Harry would have been interested in every older woman, of course – the ones he went for tended to stand out as stunningly attractive – but it was reassuring for many to feel that a teenage sex symbol still went for women of their age.

The singer Pink certainly thought so. 'It's funny following the One Direction phenomenon and what's happening with Harry Styles,' she told the *Sun*. 'Apparently he "loves" a cougar – who turns out to be a woman aged thirty-two. I just about qualify. I mean, I still feel a bit like a seventeen-year-old boy myself. I don't know if I'll ever feel any different.' She certainly wasn't the only woman who felt that way.

One Direction were still a very recent addition to the music industry, and yet such was their success that they seemed to have been around for years. That they had joined show-business aristocracy was clear when the line-up for the closing ceremony of the London Olympics was announced. Queen (the group, not the monarch), Take That, Annie Lennox, George Michael, the Pet Shop Boys and Madness would all be playing – each and every one a household name. And so, too, would One Direction, the youngest and newest stars on the night, but fast becoming as famous as the big names they were playing alongside. How had this happened? How had they come so far, so fast? And while Sir Paul McCartney was the person who closed the ceremony, some people, such as Spandau Ballet star Tony Hadley, thought One Direction should have had that honour. 'They're our biggest export at the moment, pure pop,' he told Absolute Radio. 'One Direction with the Royal Philharmonic, with about a hundred singers in a choir behind them. To me, that would have been the new generation kind of thing.'

Harry was certainly discovering you couldn't turn fame off. On a visit back to his parents, fans surrounded his Range Rover: initially he was happy to jump out and sign autographs, but when he tried to make his way home, the mob wouldn't budge, and so he was forced to dump his car at a neighbour's house and make his way on foot. The fans gave chase and Harry eventually had to jump into a Mini to drive off to meet friends. He didn't look very happy about it, but that's the price of fame.

Fascination with his love life still grew. The next person he was linked to was the Canadian singer Alyssa Reid, who he met at a gig at the Echo Arena in Liverpool. The two had dressing rooms opposite each other and Alyssa was pictured going in to say hello to the boys, before emerging clutching a telephone number. Whose was it? She wasn't going to say. 'Yes I have introduced myself . . . and I may or may not have got a phone number,' she told the *Mirror*, presumably unaware of what the trolls had in store for any girl who even hinted she knew Harry. 'But I never kiss and tell. I'm not telling you. I can't tell. I would never go for a taken man, though, so he must be one of the single ones.' That meant either Harry or Niall. Alyssa promptly started following Harry on Twitter, before adding, 'We're doing another show tomorrow so maybe I'll make a move on him then. I shouldn't have told you but I would love to cook for him – asparagus-stuffed chicken breast with Hollandaise sauce. That's one way to get a man.'

Work continued, in all its many variations. All five of the boys served food and drinks on a British Airways flight to raise money for Comic Relief: eight fans won tickets to be on board the London to Manchester trip, which was given the flight number BA1D. The flight passed without incident, with no rioting or mobbing, which came as a relief to everyone on board.

The latest person said to be interested in Harry was the

model Kate Upton, who said that he was the cutest of the five when shown a picture of him. Who would be next? Speculation was rife until Harry was seen leaving a club with another model, nineteen-year-old Cara Delevingne. They were subsequently pictured together at the exclusive Olympic VIP club Omega House in London's West End. You certainly had to credit him with energy – it was hard enough keeping up with Harry's love-life, let alone conducting it.

Harry's easy-going nature was a great part of his charm. He made no bones about the fact that he liked to spend a great deal of time naked – although interestingly, when it was suggested that the boys pose with their kit off, he suddenly became exceedingly coy. One eyewitness to Harry's penchant for getting his kit off is the singer Ed Sheeran, who was once given a lift in the boys' van. 'I turned around and Harry was stripped off completely naked, just sitting there laughing,' he told the *Daily Mirror*. 'Literally, I was just looking out the window, watching cars going past. I turn around, all the boys are kind of shocked and there's just him laughing, completely naked.' The boys might have looked shocked, but they were also getting used to it: there were plenty of stories about skinny-dipping and nakedness in hotel rooms. The wonder is that Harry has never been caught on camera in the buff.

Rumours continued to swirl about Cara, and the pair certainly seemed a good match. Cara is one of the most successful models of the moment: her agent, Sarah Doukas, has said of her, 'She has the most beautiful face and engaging personality, like her older sister Poppy. She is adorable and very talented. She has the ability to shake up the energy in a room full of stuffy people and make people ask, "Who is that girl?"' She was also extremely successful, working with the likes of Karl Lagerfeld as well as being the face of Burberry, and, surprisingly, she was almost the same age as Harry. What's not to like? In the meantime, it was announced that Lucy Horobin and her husband were going to divorce, but while Harry's name was dragged into it, sufficient time had elapsed for him not to be held directly responsible for the split. And it also helped that at the time he was mixing with girls closer to his own age.

With all this going on, it was easy to forget what the boys were actually there for: to sing. The hard-faced businessmen running the show could have been excused for going as weak at the knees as the fans, because behind the scenes, the numbers were extraordinary. In less than a year, One Direction had managed to sell 12 million singles, albums, DVDs and Blu-rays around the world, a quite astonishing amount. That comprised 8 million singles, 3 million albums and a million DVD and Blu-rays, and according to the Official Charts Company, that in turn was made up of 1.17 million One Direction singles; 660,000 copies of the album *Up All Night* and 61,000 copies of *Up All Night – The Live Tour* DVDs and Blu-rays. 'What Makes You Beautiful' alone sold nearly 700,000 copies, while 'One Thing' was in second place, with over 154,000 copies.

With these kinds of sales, the record companies were taking the boys very seriously indeed. Any fears that they might be working them too hard could be allayed by the fact that it was clearly in the record companies' interests not to kill the goose that was laying so many golden eggs. There had never been a reality-TV success story like it before: even the magnificent Susan Boyle hadn't managed to achieve so much. Never had Simon Cowell's judgement been more vindicated, and how extraordinary that it was only through the medium of a reality TV show that the boys had come together at all. That they'd had such success in the States was just the icing on the cake, and by this time it was fully expected that they would go on to even greater heights. The showbiz blogger Perez Hilton issued dire warnings that they might one day break up – as indeed has been the fate of many boy bands – but just at the moment, why would they? The boys weren't stupid. They knew they'd been handed an extraordinary opportunity, and they had no intention of blowing it now.

And the benefits of being a pop star? Well . . . even if Harry hadn't been a pop star, he would almost certainly have had no trouble attracting the ladies, because he's charming, attractive and has that indefinable air that works like a magnet on the opposite sex. Now, however, he was mixing with models and actresses, well-known beauties and some of the most sought-after women about town. He knew it and he couldn't resist talking about it – about flirting, about the chase and about what he looked for in a girl.

'The fun part is the chase, so if you speak to me, play a bit hard to get,' he told *Top of the Pops* magazine. 'I think it's attractive when someone turns you down. You don't want someone to say yes straight away, do you? I think you have to be cool to be a good flirt – and I don't think I'm very cool.'

He might not have thought so, but millions of fans disagreed. From Cheshire youth to international megastar, Harry was now one of the most successful and sought-after people on the planet. He could hardly believe his luck – and neither could his fellow band members, none of whom were lacking admirers themselves. Somehow, though, he was remaining level-headed and managing to deal with his new-found fame. What would have been fatal at this point was to let it go to his head, start acting the arrogant rock star and forget that he was part of a team who had to pull together. He didn't – none of them did. One Direction needed one another.

And so one of the most successful British pop acts in recent history began to look to the future and plan ahead. The onslaught on the United States had only just begun and there was plenty more to look forward to there. There were awards ceremonies to attend, records to record, girls to meet, places to go, people to see . . . There was no shortage of projects for Harry and the boys to concentrate on. They were leading a gilded existence: still so young, but with money, fame and even greater prospects ahead of them. They were rubbing shoulders with their showbiz peers – in August they managed a night on the lash with Tulisa – and still appreciating it. And even though the attention they received could be a little difficult to deal with, they were all sensible enough to know their life had become extraordinary.

11

Reaping the Rewards

ould One Direction get any more famous? Their star was certainly as high as it had ever been. In August 2012, they attended a film premiere, where they bumped into their former mentor, Nicole Scherzinger. When they'd met on *The X Factor*, she had been a huge star and the boys were lucky she took an interest in them; in less than two years the roles had been reversed. 'It's totally weird,' she told the *Sun*. 'I had my *Men in Black* premiere and they practically stole it. I was like, "Excuse me, I'm in the movie, scoot over, thank you." I had to remind them.' It was an incontrovertible fact that the fivesome were now massive stars.

Harry was loving every minute of it, talking about 'laddish' shopping trips to the famous Liberty's of London department store, flirting with the fans and just about everyone else and beginning to reap the rewards of the last couple of years. There was speculation that he was beginning to build up both a property portfolio and an impressive collection of motors, to say nothing of a notable array of girlfriends, too. And there was much amusement in the media as they attempted to link Harry, with his taste for older women, with *Fifty Shades of Grey*, the erotic novel by E. L. James, which had a certain appeal for middle-aged women. That a teenage member of a boy band should be giving the more mature lady her moment in the sun was strange enough, but nothing about Harry and One Direction conformed to a type.

Younger girls continued to adore them, too. One Direction appeared at the V Festival and initially mingled with everyone else in the VIP Louder Lounge, but were mobbed by so many people that they were eventually forced to retreat backstage. Only Liam stuck it out, but he was with his girlfriend, which presumably afforded some sort of protection. 'Yeah, we were mobbed a bit by the girls,' he said cheerily. 'The rest have gone off.'

Another person whose life had changed totally over the last year was Caroline Flack. She had been forced to move to a different apartment because her old one opened right onto the street, meaning she walked straight into a barrage of reporters every time she came out of the front door. There were rumours that she and Harry were back in touch, which she refused to confirm or deny, but she had returned to Twitter since the abuse had stopped. It had been a strange experience all round.

'I will live my life the way I want to,' she told the *Sun* in a defiant interview looking back over the previous year. 'And I will never judge others for living the life they want to live. The last thing I'm going to do is live my life according to anybody else. And I'm not coming off Twitter. I have fun on

Twitter. I use it for having a bit of a laugh and have got the loveliest followers. A lot of them are One Direction fans. So it's not all One Direction fans who've, y'know ... it's a minority.'

In fact, Caroline was now able to laugh about the whole experience. 'The best one I got said: "F**k you, I can't believe you're going out with my boyfriend, I hope you get eaten by an angry elephant,"' she said. 'An angry elephant? You've just got to think, these people are in front of their computers and probably don't think you even see it half the time. I just don't think anyone deserves to be bullied. That's just not on.'

Harry's friend and fellow band member Zayn couldn't have agreed more, because just as Caroline maintained that she was perfectly happy to go on tweeting, Zayn decided to leave Twitter – he had about 5 million followers – because he was getting tired of the abuse. The fans were distraught – yet again, a small minority had ruined it for everyone else. It didn't last long, though. Just one day after shutting down his account, Zayn was back. In the meantime, the fans turned their attention to Harry, though not on Twitter – a bunch of water-pistol-wielding admirers drenched him, much to everyone's amusement, although Harry later complained on Twitter that it was 'a bit nippy'.

Caroline, incidentally, appeared to be well and truly over Harry. In another interview, this time with the *Daily Star Sunday*, she was happy to return to the subject, confirming that they were indeed in touch. 'We got very close for a time but that's between me and Harry,' she said, confirming what was already very well know. 'Then we decided it was best to be just friends. Harry is adorable. He is a nice person. He was nice to me, we were nice to each other. We are still friends, he's brilliant and he is so much fun.'

Admirably, Harry seemed to be able to stay friends with his exes, because despite the fact that there were a fair few of them, nobody seemed to have a bad word to say about him. In point of fact, Harry was seen out and about everywhere. One minute he was at the Reading Festival, where he made friends with Florence Welch, who sang 'What Makes You Beautiful' as a warm-up, then he went on to G-A-Y in central London, where he was pictured larking around and having a food fight with the Radio 1 DJ Nick Grimshaw. This was topped off with a visit to the popular Funky Buddha night-club in London's Mayfair to celebrate Liam's nineteenth birthday. Harry was becoming quite the man about town.

Around about this time it was announced that 'Live While We're Young' was to be the next single; it promptly shot to the top of the pre-order charts in forty countries around the world, quite a feat for a single no one had actually heard yet. Their new album's title was also made public by Liam on Twitter – it was going to be called *Take Me Home*. Images for the cover were later released, showing the boys clambering all over a telephone box. There was also talk of doing a dance routine with the next single, something the boys had never got properly into. It was a wise move: if they wanted to emulate the great Take That, then at some point they were going to have to learn how to hoof it.

Harry, meanwhile, had become rather fond of tattoos, and had just had a new one – '17 Black' – tattooed on his collarbone. The band's management were relaxed about it: they kept a sharp eye on the band's image, but so far Harry had been discreet enough to get away with it. Along with the rest of the boys, he was turning into a comic character – literally. They had become animations in a series of biography comics called *Fame*, although observers noted that the famous floppy hair didn't appear quite as glorious as it was in real life. The five of them also signed a deal with Pepsi, following in the footsteps of Madonna, Michael Jackson, David Beckham and Britney Spears, guaranteeing more millions would soon be flowing into their bank accounts.

In September 2012, the controversy surrounding the name of the group came to a conclusion, with the British One Direction winning the right to keep their name. Simon Cowell's entertainment company Syco had put in a counterclaim to the effect that the US outfit was trying to make money from the British group's success, forcing the American group to back down. One Direction won the right to keep their name, while the US band changed its moniker to Unchartered Shores.

Both groups put out press releases saying they were happy with the outcome, while the US band revealed that they had been the subject of death threats and hate mail from One Direction fans. No one was particularly surprised – given the internet treatment dished out to anyone who spoke out against the band, there was bound to have been some kind of backlash. The triumph was particularly close to Harry's heart; it was he who had come up with the name, after all, and he had been particularly insistent that they shouldn't give it up. Now he had been vindicated. The name was theirs to keep and move on with. Their management was relieved, too. To change names at this late stage, and after such astonishing success, would have been a marketing nightmare.

Just a couple of days later, the boys were utterly triumphant at the MTV Video Music Awards. They took home more awards than anyone else on the night, trumping The Wanted, and being named as Best New Artist, Best Pop Video and Most Shareworthy Video. Harry was utterly overwhelmed: 'This has been unbelievable,' he said. 'This was our favourite performance. For us to be here in the first place is amazing, and to perform and win three VMAs is amazing.' Who could blame him for being so overwhelmed? The MTV awards are the most famous in the business, rewarding the very best in the profession, and One Direction had now been publicly acclaimed by their peers. Other winners that year included Rihanna, Chris Brown, Coldplay and Lil Wayne – in other words, some of the hottest acts out there. And One Direction had topped them all.

Unsurprisingly, they all felt overawed. 'We've grown up watching this show, and for us to even be here is an honour,' said Niall. Their performance that night had provoked more screams than any other, with even the US gymnastics team singing along; an absolutely delighted Simon Cowell tweeted, 'Congratulations 1D. I'm very proud of you. Celebrate!' It was as big a triumph for Cowell as it was for One Direction. Not only did his music company stand to benefit from the even bigger sales that would inevitably follow; it consolidated his reputation as one of the most influential men in the entertainment industry. After this, any thought of Simon taking a back seat when choosing future acts was banished: he had probably never made a better decision.

The boys were nice enough not to crow about it, but The Wanted had been up for the MTV New Artist award, too. In the end they took it in good part, went on stage to present a prize to Nicki Minaj and, well away from the cameras, shook hands with all the One Direction boys. There did indeed seem to be room for both groups and their markedly different styles, though there was really no question as to which was the most popular band at the time.

The MTV awards ceremony was held in Los Angeles, and the next day Zayn was seen hobbling about on crutches, while Harry rented a black Ferrari and drove it around town. Back in London, he took possession of his next car, a vintage E-type Jaguar, the latest addition to a collection that now included a Porsche, an Audi and a Range Rover. The critics pouted – all that money! – but why not? When David Beckham first became famous he, too, splashed out on a few motors, and given that Harry was also spending his money on bricks and mortar, surely he should be allowed to spend some of the fruits of his success on something frivolous.

Practically every move Harry made went public: in an age of camera phones and Twitter, very little remains private for long. This created its own strains, and one person who knew exactly what that felt like was Robbie Williams. Now a positive veteran at thirty-eight, he felt that in many ways it had been easier being a high-profile pop star in his day.

'It's only natural a lad in a boy band will be compared to me at some point,' he said in an interview with the *Sun*, sounding a little like a younger version of Sir Paul McCartney. 'Everybody is a ladies' man or a man's man, whatever your persuasion might be. He's just having a nice time. I see Harry through bitter-getting-old-and-married-and-can't-do-all-of-that-any-more eyes. Also, I've got a lot of love for him and One Direction. On the pie chart, the love outweighs the bitterness – but the bitterness is in there, too.'

Robbie was clearly joking, but he went on to make a serious point. 'I feel a bit for Harry,' he said. 'At his age I was in this lilywhite boy band, Take That. But I was meeting up with mates, jumping out of the tour bus and into a Transit van at motorway service stations all around the country. Whenever I had the chance to go clubbing, I went. I'd go to Miss Moneypenny's in Birmingham, I'd go to the Hacienda in Manchester. It's not a secret any more, but I would get off my face and have complete anonymity. No one had a camera phone so I could go and enjoy myself properly. Harry is finding out it's not so easy for him.'

Indeed it was not. And not only did Harry risk being photographed every time he stepped outside, there were all sorts of new challenges to contend with that pop stars in an earlier age wouldn't have had to worry about. It wasn't just the girls who associated with the band that received death threats; the five boys themselves did, too. They needed a constant security presence, and not just because of the deranged; the devoted fans could prove a danger, too – their sheer force of numbers could easily turn into a crush. Social media only exacerbated the situation: a sighting of one of the boys could go viral within seconds, prompting fans in the area to come out and see their heroes, and a crowd turning, within moments, into a mob. Even the odd shopping trip had to be carefully patrolled and monitored these days.

Sometimes the attention surrounding the boys turned into a farce. Sarah Cox, a thirty-seven-year-old cleaner from Melksham, Wiltshire, was a little bemused when she found herself bombarded with love messages after receiving a new phone. It subsequently emerged that the phone, a BlackBerry Bold, wasn't exactly new; it was a reconditioned model that had previously belonged to one Niall Horan, and although Niall had returned it within fourteen days, fans had got hold of his number and passed it around the world. Some simply refused to believe that it no longer belonged to Niall and accused Sarah of stealing it. In the end, the company that had issued the phone, O2, was forced to give Sarah another handset.

On the upside, their showbiz life continued. James Corden was getting married, and his best man, Ben Winston, persuaded the whole of One Direction, alongside Sir Paul McCartney, Robbie Williams, Gary Barlow and Snow Patrol, to play cameo roles in a video, each recording a line from a song James wrote when he was a teenager. Harry also turned up at the Burberry show during London Fashion Week, where he was pictured sitting next to the burlesque artist Dita Von Teese – to the disappointment of the media, they didn't end up hooking up, though. She would have been a cougar to write about. Also present were Sir Jonathan Ive of Apple and tennis star Andy Murray, leading to speculation that Burberry wanted them all present to boost its international image. To put it in a nutshell: Harry was capable of 'shifting product', be it through record sales, endorsement deals or just turning up to look at the catwalk.

Of course, there was another reason Harry turned up at Burberry, and that was Cara Delevingne. She was modelling in the show, and although neither of them had confirmed or denied being involved, onlookers couldn't help but notice Harry's grin every time Cara appeared. Cara herself had responded to the inevitable Twitter approaches by saying, 'Please just stop guessing, you don't need to know,' but it was unlikely that would satisfy anyone. The whole world couldn't stop speculating about Harry and his love-life – hence the continuing interest in Caroline Flack nine months after their fling ended – and there was no denying that Harry and Cara made a handsome couple. These days, however, Harry was learning to be a little more discreet. He had been so public with his flirting before – telling Lucy on-air that she looked lovely, or holding up a picture of Kim Kardashian with 'call me maybe' written across it – all of which had fuelled the

Fame is something of a rollercoaster ride, but the boys
make sure to keep each other grounded.

After this picture of
Harry and Emma
Ostilly was released, the
model was sent such
abusive messages that
she was forced to delete
her Twitter account.

Harry Styles reveals exactly what makes him beautiful on
a yacht in Chinaman's Beach, Sydney.

Their biggest gig yet, 1D join the cream of British talent at the Olympics Closing Ceremony.

Not so good-looking any more . . . the other band members push Harry's face into a cake at the *Elvis Duran and the Morning Show*, made to congratulate them on breaking the US.

The girls go wild for Harry at the MTV Video and Music Awards.

One Direction pick up one of their three MTV awards, crowning their arrival on the US pop scene.

He kissed a girl and he liked it . . . Katy Perry has a unique way
of congratulating Harry on his award.

Papped! Harry and Taylor Swift
were spotted on a romantic stroll
through Central Park after their
visit to its famous zoo.

The inseparable Harry and Taylor can't escape the press as they continue dating.

Harry confesses he channels Chris Martin on stage, mimicking his jig.

One Direction perform on the series finale of *X Factor USA*, showing how far they've evolved since they first appeared on an *X Factor* stage.

Larking around backstage, despite their success they're still the easy-going guys they always were.

Harry Stylish! He knows how to win a girl's heart,
and Harry has won them across the globe.

flames of speculation, but he was beginning to realize that life would be a lot easier if he kept more under wraps.

Clearly he wasn't ready to settle down just yet. Pixie Geldof celebrated her birthday by meeting friends in a karaoke bar, Lucky Voice, in London's Soho: also present were Harry and Alexa Chung. Harry and Alexa flirted heavily all evening, and left together in a taxi, accompanied by Pixie and her boyfriend; some people got hold of the wrong end of the stick, however, and thought Harry and Pixie were an item. The tweets began, but Pixie was totally unmoved: 'Had the greatest birthday!' she tweeted. 'Dinner, karaoke! Then a late night singsong by a piano!' Harry sang the Justin Bieber number, 'Boyfriend', and rarely can a song have been more appropriate. The whole world – or at least a sizeable female portion of it – wanted Harry to be their boyfriend. The boy couldn't help it: he had turned into one of the most popular objects of desire in the world.

A new biography of Simon Cowell had also recently appeared. Written by Tom Bower, with Cowell's tacit approval, it mainly attracted attention for the revelations about Simon's love-life, in particular his relationship with Dannii Minogue and his feelings for Cheryl Cole. What initially went unnoticed was an even more extraordinary piece of news: the full extent of One Direction's earnings over the past year. Bower estimated that the boys had earned almost £100 million for themselves, and that did not include the £200 million they were estimated to have earned for Cowell and Sony. One

Direction were Cowell's new Westlife, he said, adding that they had earned nearly £100 million from songs, publishing, discs, DVDs, merchandising and endorsements. *Up All Night* had sold five million copies alone, they had merchandising deals with Nokia, Pokémon and Hasbro, and the recent Pepsi link-up was thought to be worth about £11 million. Then there were three books, all of which had topped the bestseller lists, a world tour and their 2011 calendar, which had been the best-selling ever. No wonder the boys were beginning to splash out on lavish houses and, in Harry's case, several garages full of expensive cars.

Harry continued to enjoy himself hugely, and was spotted flirting with the thirty-seven-year-old Australian singer Natalie Imbruglia at James Corden's wedding reception at Babington House, near Frome in Somerset. Both were staying in the hotel and there were reports, which both resolutely refused to confirm, that not only did they appear at breakfast together, they were also the subject of some whooping and hollering from the other guests when they emerged. When approached by a reporter to ask if it was true, Natalie was not forthcoming: 'Why are you asking me? Go ask him,' she said. The boys went on to play the iTunes festival at the Roundhouse in London, and onlookers observed a grin on Harry's face as they performed 'Torn', which just happened to be a hit song by Natalie Imbruglia. Harry's friend Nick Grimshaw, who was in the audience, did nothing to dampen speculation when he tweeted, 'They are doing a cover of "Torn" by Natalie Imbruglia. LOLLLLZZZZ.'

Harry's antics did nothing to discourage the fans, who were more devoted than ever, so much so that seating had to be put in the Roundhouse for safety reasons, to avoid anyone getting crushed in the melee. Apart from 'Torn', they went through their growing repertoire, which included 'Gotta Be You', 'What Makes You Beautiful', 'One Thing' and 'Na Na Na', as well as telling the fans how much they enjoyed being back in London. They had, after all, spent a great deal of time abroad, especially in the United States. On the same day they premiered their new single 'Live While We're Young' and its accompanying video – the release was earlier than planned, but was deemed necessary as a poor-quality version had been leaked online.

'Live While We're Young', which was a Top 10 hit in fifteen countries, debuting at number three in the United States, the second highest position any UK act had debuted at (the first was Sir Elton John, who went in at number one with 'Candle In The Wind' in 1997), came from the same stable as their previous hits. Written by Rami Yacoub, Carl Falk and Savan Kotecha, and produced by Yacoub and Falk, it's an upbeat celebration of the joys of youth. On the whole it got positive reviews: Robert Copsey of *Digital Spy* gave it four out of five stars, saying, 'It's a little different from what we've heard before – but when you're the world's biggest boy band, it's no bad thing.'

Mikael Wood of the *Los Angeles Times* said it was a 'characteristically peppy piece of high-gloss party pop', while Andrew Unterberger of *Popdust* wrote that 'the song is smart to swipe the guitar-only opening pattern from The Clash's "Should I Stay Or Should I Go?" – akin to "What Makes You Beautiful" lifting the "Summer Nights" beginning – calling on pop history to get you excited for the song before you even really realize why.'

Sylvie Lesas of *Evigshed Magazine* gave it a rating of five out of five stars and said it was 'upbeat, fun and very fresh', adding that 'radios are going to love it'. Chris Younie of *4Music* called it 'insanely catchy', and *MSN Music*'s Tina Hart noted the utilization of elements of One Direction's 'What Makes You Beautiful' and 'One Thing', which is a 'massive pop win . . . It's fun, pure unadulterated pop and I like it.'

The accompanying video, which was directed by Vaughan Amell, was shot in Tunbridge Wells, in the picturesque county of Kent, and had the boys larking about in a camping setting, messing about in boats on a lake, taking part in a football match and pool party and generally having fun. It broke the Vevo record for having the most views with 8.24 million hits, beating the previous record, which was held by Justin Bieber's 'Boyfriend' (he subsequently got it back again with 'Beauty and a Beat'). The video garnered generous reviews for being sunny, good-natured and fun. It was an 'epic summer adventure,' said the *Huffington Post*, 'from a camping trip to the ultimate beach party'.

Live While We're Young' was also featured in a Pepsi TV commercial, which showed Harry and the American football player Drew Brees arguing about who gets a can of the drink. The two show off their achievements and Niall then tells

Drew he can join One Direction if he gives Harry the can. It ends with Drew joining in and singing part of 'Live While We're Young'. This also got good reviews and allowed the boys to show that they had a hitherto undiscovered gift for comedy. 'The brand-new commercial not only allows the group to show off their funny bones,' wrote Jocelyn Vena of *MTV*, who thought the ad was comedic, 'it also serves as a reminder that their new album *Take Me Home*, featuring "LWWY", is only a month away from dropping.' Well, quite.

12
Nothing Succeeds Like Success

The boys just couldn't stop winning. They turned up at the Radio 1 Teen Awards, where they picked up Best British Single for 'One Thing', Best British Album and Best British Music Act. Somewhat inexplicably, they were trailing a life-size cardboard cutout of Prince Harry, who was in the news at that point because he'd somewhat unwisely disrobed in front of a group of new friends in Las Vegas, and the subsequent photographs had been passed around the world. Were the boys displaying solidarity with him? Certainly Prince Harry's fun-loving persona was very much like them – the prince and One Direction's most popular member even shared a name, and comparisons between the two seemed apt. 'They were getting a bit giddy and clearly worship Harry's antics in Vegas,' said a bystander. And why not? They were all lads out to have a good time. And so was someone else attending the awards that year: Taylor Swift. However, she had a boyfriend at the time, so reports that she and Harry were getting on famously clearly showed them just as friends.

Just for once, though, the boys let their guard slip that

night and welcomed a comparison with the Fab Four. 'We watched that film of The Beatles when they first touched down in America and we saw a real likeness with our personalities,' said Harry.

'They loved having a laugh like us,' added Niall.

Another sign of the road they'd travelled came when Harry admitted that they could no longer decide which side of the Atlantic was home. 'When we're in America I'd say home is London, and when we're back here we feel like home is there,' he said. 'It's a bit weird.' It's a commonplace feeling amongst international entertainers, who have to learn to make home wherever they are at any given time.

Harry continued to be linked with just about every girl he was pictured with, but, according to his friend Will Sweeney, he was getting tired of playing the field. 'Harry is looking for a relationship,' Will told the *Sun*. 'He's always going to parties with different girls, but it's lonely for him and not what he wants. The girls are just there for the night. You have fun but that's the end of it.'

Meanwhile, one of his exes was still being teased about their past. The latest series of *The X Factor* was airing, and Caroline was hosting *The Xtra Factor* again on ITV2. In one episode, screened in September, footage was shown of Caroline and Louis Walsh jokingly 'getting married' in Las Vegas.

'Louis, I want a divorce,' Caroline declared.

'OK,' said Louis immediately.

'As I'm your wife, I'm entitled to half of everything you

own, so I'll take half of Westlife,' said Caroline. 'I'll take Kian and Mark. And also I want John of Jedward.'

'Do I get a slice of One Direction?' Louis asked coyly.

'It was a great comeback,' Caroline later admitted.

Over on the main show, the boys made an appearance – after all, they owed everything to the series that had aired two years earlier. A lot had changed since then. Then they were nobodies and now they were global superstars. It brought it home just how far they had come. 'It's really weird being back on the *X Factor* stage,' said Louis, wonderingly, to the *Sun*. 'Walking through those doors always made us nervous and it kinda feels like you're back in the competition. Being interviewed by Dermot O'Leary brings all the old nerves back. We would love to come back and perform before Christmas. *The X Factor* is our home and we love it.' Harry bumped into Caroline when they were in situ – but was seen leaving with someone else. He was, however, just as keen as Caroline to emphasize that they still got on fine: 'We still have a lot of the same friends and we're fine,' he said. 'There seems to be the idea that every time we meet we argue, but we don't.'

One Direction were now firmly part of the cultural landscape. It was announced that Penguin's teen imprint Razorbill was to publish a book called *Loving the Band* by sixteen-year-old Emily Baker: it was actually based on fanfiction and was inspired by One Direction, so the boys had become a muse for aspiring authors. 'We're online all the time looking for new writers through various different means,' said Lindsey Heaven, senior fiction editor at Razorbill. 'With fan-fiction there's already a fan base established, which is fantastic. I think people are generally more aware of the new channels that are opening up, and any serious publisher would be completely open to writing from many different sources, and because fan-fiction is more popular than ever, it's worth taking notice of.' *Fifty Shades of Grey* was the most famous such work to date, since it was originally based on the *Twilight* series – now the boys were providing inspiration themselves. Their influence, it seems, had moved far beyond the music industry, and would go further still.

Back on *The Xtra Factor*, Caroline was still getting stick: she had 'big news,' she told Louis.

'Is it that you like older men?' Louis replied.

Meanwhile, gossip about Taylor Swift intensified. There were rumours that while she was in the UK she'd made plans to have dinner with a member of One Direction, but when news of the plans leaked out, she cancelled. The question is, which member? 'It wasn't me,' said Harry firmly. And then there was the fact that Taylor had a boyfriend – Conor Kennedy. It was all very strange. In the end she was whisked off in her private jet from Luton airport, though there were plans afoot for her to return to the UK soon . . .

One Direction's promotional work continued, this time with a deal to launch toothpaste and toothbrushes with Colgate. Some people thought it a little strange, but it certainly fitted with their squeaky-clean personalities. There was a further distraction from what was really going on – or beginning to – when it was rumoured that Harry was angling for an introduction to Lisa Marie Presley, who had relocated to the south of England. In actual fact, the seeds of a very different relationship had been sown. Harry had been marked out as a ladies' man for some time now and had yet to be really serious about anyone. All that was about to change.

Speculation about his love-life was overshadowed by news from the United States: 'Live While We're Young' had just entered the charts and sold 341,000 in the first week, soaring to the top spot. Even after their proven success in the United States, this was an astonishing performance that boded extremely well for their next album. They had been around for a while now and needed to prove they had staying power – it was beginning to look as if they did.

The promotional appearances continued, with the boys turning up in Dublin, where they were pursued by the usual hordes of fans – not that they appeared to mind. Niall always came into his own on the Irish trips, as it was a return to his homeland, and the others were clearly having just as much fun as he was. Harry, Louis and Liam all got new tattoos, and the boys did a brief tour of some of the city's hottest night-clubs, before appearing on the *Late Late Show*, thrilling the fans once more.

As the promotional game moved on, Liam let slip that they were under a fair degree of pressure. 'I think so. It's the second album syndrome thing – or whatever they call it,' he said. 'But we didn't want to change it up too much. We wanted to keep it quite similar but make a few subtle differences.

As we have got older we want the music to grow up with us. But it's a lot more live-sounding. The songs are about things that have happened in our own experiences.' In the meantime there were raised eyebrows when the boys confessed to raiding their minibars in the hotel rooms in the United States, where they were all still technically too young to drink, and there was further tension when Zayn's appearance on a Canadian radio station was suddenly cancelled. The reason appeared to be because there was a list of questions he said he wouldn't answer and the DJ took umbrage, but in truth, considering that one of those questions was how One Direction got their name, he was probably bored with being asked the same things all the time. Whatever the reason, it was in everyone's interests to keep the show on the road, so they all persevered.

They could scarcely be called the elder statesmen of the showbiz world, but One Direction had certainly become something other aspiring boy bands looked up to. The current series of *The X Factor* had thrown up another hopeful boy band called Union J, who seemed rather overwhelmed when they met up with One Direction. Union J's George Shelley had been compared to Harry and was seen deep in conversation with his role model: what advice did Harry dish out? 'Never cut your curls,' was the answer.

All of the Union J boys seemed a little star-struck: 'It was awesome to meet them as they've been in the same position we're in now a couple of years ago,' they said. Liam, meanwhile, told them, 'Just go out there and have fun.' Louis counselled, 'Just be yourselves.' It seemed like only a few weeks earlier that Robbie Williams had been passing on boy-band wisdom to newcomers One Direction – and indeed, it really hadn't been long. Things move fast on Planet Showbiz.

Harry and George had got on extremely well. 'Harry and George swapped numbers as the two groups are bound to start bumping into each other around the scene,' a witness to the meeting told the *Daily Mirror*. 'Harry sees a lot of himself in George, so he wanted to pass on a jokey text revealing his secret, which is why he told him never to cut his curls as he reckons his hair makes him such a hit with the ladies. George was laughing and showed the text to a couple of people, but I'd say there's no way he'll be going for any drastic haircuts from now on.' It was sound advice. Not since Samson had anyone derived quite so much strength from their hair.

It was announced that One Direction had won a public poll for Best UK and Ireland Act, which would be presented at the following month's MTV European Music Awards. Meanwhile, Union J suddenly found the comparison with One Direction was working against them when Louis Walsh claimed that Simon Cowell was concerned the new boys were a threat to his more established act, so was backing away from them. 'He knows Union J are a threat to One Direction, so he's not going to say much about them,' Louis stormed to the *Daily Star*. In truth, it was very unlikely he had anything to worry about as the One Direction boys were going from strength to strength. Toymaker Hasbro certainly thought so – although their profits had fallen in the three months to October 2012, sales of girls' toys were on the increase and the firm's bosses were hoping their One Direction dolls would do well over the Christmas period. Harry's, in particular, was expected to sell well.

Union J took the spat in their stride, understanding it for what it was, namely a bid to drum up publicity for the show. 'I loved that Simon was threatened by us. I rang Louis straight away and asked what he'd said,' related Union J member Jaymi Hensley. 'Louis said Simon was threatened because he has a boy band this year who could topple his. Simon has got the groups on US *X Factor*, so he's trying to get his own new One Direction from America. But Louis has got his game face on this year, so I think there is an extra bit of competition between Simon and Louis. Louis has told us he's determined to win. It's nice that we are still on Simon's radar, even though he isn't on the show this year.'

After the year they'd had, it was hardly surprising that One Direction were the highest new entry at number five in a rich list of British stars: their personal earnings were now over £5 million each, something they had accomplished in the space of less than a year. All the boys were splashing out on properties now, with Harry buying a house in north London, home of the famous Primrose Hill set.

Everyone wanted to be associated with One Direction, even well-established, famous stars. Robbie Williams gave another interview in which he mentioned them, relating that in the early days of Take That, he and Gary Barlow had had a very love/hate relationship, and that he suspected something similar was going on with the boys. If it was, though, they certainly weren't showing it: his fellow band members had never shown any jealousy about the fact that Harry continued to be the most popular one of the five. Then again, they got such a lot of attention, with the other four boys having their own devoted fans, that there wasn't a great deal to be jealous of.

Another person happy to talk about meeting them was none other than Kylie Minogue. 'I was drinking with One Direction at James Corden's wedding,' she told the *Sunday Mirror*, adding the advice she had passed on to them. 'I was hanging with the teens. I can definitely see what their appeal is and they are adorable and nice guys. And they have the songs to back it all up. I don't know what the secret formula is and I haven't always got it right, but you have to take risks and learn who you are. I didn't always know who I was at the beginning and you need to find your strengths and work on your weaknesses.'

Kylie was one woman Harry didn't end up with – she, too, had a boyfriend – but he made no bones about his fondness for the fairer sex. 'I'm eighteen, I don't love older women, I just love women. Sometimes I flirt without meaning to,' he protested. 'Perhaps it's just how I was meant to be. I've got a good seduction routine which I execute very well.' That much was obvious to everyone, but the question remained: who was next?

It was announced that the boys were to sing at the Royal

Variety Performance, along with the likes of Robbie Williams, Kylie Minogue, Rod Stewart, Alicia Keys and Girls Aloud. They gave an interview for *Vogue*, in which Harry told the magazine, 'You're never going to get used to people screaming at you. There's a lot of things that come with the life you could get lost in. But you have to let it be what it is. I've learnt not to take everything too seriously.'

That interview – in *Vogue* itself, not *Teen Vogue*, which the boys also appeared in – was another indicator of their elevated status. The boys weren't pictured in their usual larking-around style; instead they came across as rather solemn, shot in black and white. The photographer was Patrick Demarchelier, one of the most famous photographers in the world, and he was unlikely to start snapping the shutters unless his subjects were considered sufficiently important. Alexa Chung was quoted in the article: 'They're no Beatles, obviously, but it's nice to see a boy band dress well for a change,' she said. 'They remind me of a box of puppies at Christmas – each one more adorable than the next.' It was a telling insight into the world they now inhabited: Harry confessed to enjoying photo-shoots, and having a love for fashion – hence that appearance at Burberry – and he also seemed extremely comfortable with his growing fame.

The piece was written by Jo Ellison, and she did a brilliant job of explaining Harry's appeal. 'If you have heard nothing whatsoever of One Direction you have probably heard of Harry Styles, the hazel-eyed, mop-topped, bedimpled lead singer and baby of the group, with whom the whole world has fallen in love,' she said. 'Harry, an Aquarian who hails from the village of Holmes Chapel in Cheshire. Harry, whose delightful scowl of petulant confusion, like a teddy bear trying to do trigonometry, has skewered millions of fluttering hearts, and has wooed scores of women . . . Harry, whose favourite food is tacos, who hates mayonnaise . . .' Harry, who had won the world over and was clearly going to carry on doing so.

During the shoot, the boys posed with the lovely twenty-two-year-old model Edie Campbell. Almost inevitably, she promptly became the subject of Twitter abuse, despite the fact that she had a boyfriend, Otis Ferry, the son of Bryan Ferry. Trolls issued threats, telling her not to touch Harry again, although she handled the situation with remarkable aplomb. 'As long as they don't appear at my door with fire-lit torches, I reckon I can handle it,' she said.

A young lady called Amy Green was having a similar problem, although it involved Niall rather than Harry. Amy, a drama student, had just become Niall's girlfriend, leading to a flood of abuse on Twitter: 'Ignore the haters,' Niall advised her. The boys quite regularly spoke out against trolling – they were even occasionally the subject of it themselves – but nothing they did could solve the problem. People who spent any time with them, especially women, just had to develop a very thick skin.

The same month, the boys also appeared on the cover of *Teen Vogue*, the thought being, presumably, that they could cater to fans in all age ranges. Again Harry came across as modest and charming – and in many ways he was unable to believe his luck. 'One time, a girl dropped her phone in my pocket,' he said, 'and I found it and was like, "There you go." And she said, "If you'd had my phone, you'd have had to meet up with me to give it back." It's nice to have people go to these lengths for you, but sometimes it's hard to understand, because we're just guys. We're guys who would be at your school, who got this amazing opportunity.' It was an accurate self-assessment, and one that did him credit. Many stars have tasted success very young and let it go straight to their heads, and in that the seeds of self-destruction are sown. Harry and the boys were going in the opposite direction: the more popular and sought-after they became, the more determined they were to hang on to what was normal about them. They genuinely couldn't understand the furore they generated: they were simply five normal boys from middle Britain who happened to have done well on a television reality show. But whether or not they encouraged it, their star just carried on getting bigger and bigger. It was no longer a case of fighting for recognition: they were now five of the most famous faces in the world.

Still they didn't let it go to their heads. Each of the boys came across as down-to-earth, fully aware of how lucky he was and even, as much as anyone could be in that position, modest. There was no preening, no sense of 'I deserve it'. Somehow, against all the odds, a group of very young men had conquered the world and managed to keep their feet on the ground.

They were, however, beginning to display the odd war

wound. With a lengthy world tour coming up, the boys needed to be at the peak of fitness and, well, they weren't. Harry had a bad back, for which he was doing Pilates; Zayn had been on crutches after getting hurt partying; Liam had just suffered a broken toe after a laptop fell on it, and Niall had dislocated his knee, not once, not twice, but fourteen times. They were also preparing to release a new single, 'Little Things', and as if that weren't enough, they had once again soared to the top of the calendar charts, with HMV reporting that they were the bestselling calendar for 2013, ahead of both Justin Bieber and Tom Daley.

As well as spending some of his new-found wealth on himself, Harry also spent some on buying a new house for his mother and step-father: the constant presence of admirers outside the old family home had become too much to deal with and somewhere more secluded was needed. In the meantime, the publicity offensive continued. Just as they had stepped away from their normal image for the dark and moody photo-shoot for *Vogue*, so the boys now posed for *Wonderland* magazine, looking for all the world as if they'd just stepped out of the 1950s. Each of them was wearing a striped shirt and pullover, and each was cradling a blond Labrador puppy. It was an image designed to melt the heart of the onlooker, and it worked – and when you discovered that the puppies were in fact trainee Guide Dogs, the image was even more adorable. The boys were keen to insist, however, that they weren't going to confirm to a boy-band stereotype by all dressing the same way: this was a one-off.

Harry and the rest of One Direction were also on the cover of *Cosmopolitan* that month – the first all-male cover picture in the magazine's forty-year history – but when you're hot, you're hot and people didn't come much hotter than Harry and his band members at that moment. *Cosmo* quizzed Harry on his ideal girl, to which he replied, 'I find ambition really attractive – if someone's good at something they love doing. I want someone who is driven.' As it happened, he almost certainly had someone in mind. The rest of the world hadn't quite cottoned on to it yet, but it seemed it was only a matter of time. He also added in the interview, 'I feel so lucky to be in this position. I'm not entitled to get annoyed. I'm not half as busy as they make out! The way it's portrayed is that I only see women in a sexual way, but I grew up with just my mum and sister, so I respect women a lot.' That, it seemed, was the secret of his success as a ladies man, but things were about to change.

Harry had had quite a few flings, some longer than others, and had made quite a reputation for himself as a lothario, although to be fair most young men in his position would have done exactly the same. It seemed that now, though, Harry was ready for a proper relationship, and he was on the cusp of starting it, as the rest of the world was about to witness. So who was the lucky lady? Well, she might be an older woman, but not *too* much older, and it was someone who would be able to understand exactly the sort of pressures Harry was under, because she was experiencing them, too. She was almost as famous as Harry, and together the two of them were going to become one of the most high-profile couples in the world of entertainment. In no time, they were to be pictured everywhere, spending as much time together as possible, given their hugely busy schedules and global commitments. Harry would even speak publicly about being in love, something he'd never done before. And the name of the woman to bring about such a change in him? Taylor Swift.

13

Taylor Who?

The date was 13 December 1989. Scott Kingsley Swift, a financial adviser at the US giant Merrill Lynch, and his wife Andrea, who had previously been a mutual fund marketing executive and was now a housewife, were celebrating the birth of their first child. She was a bonny baby girl, much loved and much anticipated by her doting parents, who named their new bundle of joy Taylor Alison Swift. The slightly unusual name was because Andrea believed a gender-neutral moniker would help her daughter found a successful business career, but more pertinently, perhaps, Taylor was named after the singer James Taylor. Would the knowledge of this have some bearing on her future career? Singing talent clearly ran in the family, as Taylor's grandmother Marjorie Finlay was an opera singer. 'I can remember her singing, the thrill of it,' Taylor told *Readingeagle.com*. 'She was one of my first inspirations.'

The couple went on to have another child, Austin, and the family lived on an eleven-acre Christmas tree farm in Montgomery County, Pennsylvania. It was a privileged existence: the family owned several horses and a pony, and Taylor was first put on a horse at the age of nine months. She grew up loving riding, as well as amateur dramatics, which she started participating in when she was nine. In her early years she went to preschool and kindergarten at the Alvernia Montessori School, which was run by Franciscan nuns, before moving on to the prestigious Wyndcroft School.

When Taylor was nine, the family moved to Wyomissing, Pennsylvania, where she attended the West Reading Elementary Centre and the Wyomissing Area Junior/Senior High School. Holidays were spent at her parents' second home in Stone Harbour, New Jersey – a pretty idyllic place. 'We lived on this basin where all this magical stuff would happen,' she told American *Vogue* (Harry wasn't the only one to feature in the glossies). 'One time a dolphin swam into our basin. We had this family of otters that would live on our dock at night. We'd turn the light on and you'd see them, you know, hanging out, just being otters. And then one summer, there was a shark that washed up on our dock. I ended up writing a novel that summer because I wouldn't go in the water. I locked myself in the den and wrote a book when I was fourteen because of a shark!'

At the same time, Taylor was becoming seriously interested in the world of show business. She was a member of the Berks Youth Theatre Academy and took part in productions of *Grease*, *Annie*, *Bye Bye Birdie* and *The Sound of Music*, as well as travelling to New York for vocal and acting lessons. She started going for auditions, too, but when she didn't get anywhere, Taylor became increasingly interested in country music, and started doing the rounds of festivals and fairs. When she was eleven, she won a local talent competition with a rendition of LeAnn Rimes's 'Big Deal'. This led to an appearance as the opening act for Charlie Daniels at a Strausstown amphitheater, and it started to become clear in which direction her future lay.

Right from the start, Taylor transformed her experiences into music. In later years, after she'd made a name for herself, she attracted a great deal of praise for the honesty of her lyrics, addressing the subjects that occupy so many teenage girls, but it dated back to her pre-teens, when she translated her everyday life into the stuff of her songs. 'The people around me provided all the inspiration I needed,' she told *Readingeagle.com*. 'Everything I wrote came from that experience, what I observed happening around me.' At the time, of course, it was all a child's perception of events, although in time, as we'll see later, it was to include observations about her love-life.

Showing the kind of precociousness that made Harry look like a late developer, Taylor was still just eleven when she persuaded her mother to take her to Nashville, Tennessee, the home of country music, where she delivered a demo tape to every record label she could think of. She didn't get anywhere initially but, showing extraordinary initiative for such a young girl, she started to think of ways to make herself stand out, including singing 'The Star Spangled Banner' at sporting events, 'because it was a way to get in front of 20,000 people without having a record deal.' She learned how to play the guitar and, having previously won a poetry con-test, turned her hand to songwriting. She got a manager, Dan Dymtrow, started modelling for Abercrombie & Fitch in their 'Rising Stars' campaign and, after a performance at an RCA Records showcase, finally landed an artist develop-ment deal.

By this stage, it was pretty obvious to everyone that Taylor was an extraordinary child, and so it was that when she was fourteen, the entire family relocated to Hendersonville, Ten-nessee, with Scott transferring to Merrill Lynch's Nashville office. 'My parents saw that I was so obsessed that I wasn't going to drop it, that it wasn't some adolescent phase,' she told *Marie Claire*. 'My parents were thrown into this – they never had any desire for me to do music.' Taylor initially attended Hendersonville High School, but as performing duties got in the way of her schooling, she transferred to the Aaron Academy, which meant she could be home-schooled. It should come as no surprise to anyone that she completed her final two years of coursework in just twelve months.

Taylor eventually signed to Big Machine Records and became the youngest ever songwriter hired by the Sony/ATV Music publishing house. Her debut album in 2006, entitled *Taylor Swift*, was an immediate success and she set about breaking records in much the way that Harry and One Dir-ection would a few years later: her third single, 'Our Song', made her the youngest person to single-handedly write and perform a number-one song in the country charts. Her second album, *Fearless*, released in 2008, won four Grammy awards, and two more albums followed. Taylor also became the youngest ever winner of Album of the Year (for *Fearless*), as well as becoming the first ever female artist to have two albums that sold over a million the week they were released. She was also the first country music artist to win an MTV Video Music Award for 'You Belong With Me' – an event made controversial by Kanye West interrupting her acceptance speech. While upsetting for Taylor at the time, the incident made international headlines and did nothing to harm her global profile. In 2011, *Billboard* named her Woman of the Year. Harry wasn't kidding when he said he was attracted to ambitious, driven women: you don't get much more ambitious and driven than this.

Since then, Taylor has been honoured by the Nashville Songwriters Association and the Songwriters Hall of Fame; she has won six Grammy Awards, eleven American Music Awards, seven Country Music Association Awards, six Academy of Country Music Awards and thirteen BMI Awards. She has sold over 22 million albums worldwide and 51.1 million digital downloads in the United States, as of 2012. She has also appeared as an actress in the crime drama *CSI* (2009), the ensemble comedy *Valentine's Day* (2010) and the animated film *The Lorax* (2012). The list of her achievements is simply endless and Forbes estimates that she is currently worth over $165 million.

As well as career success, Taylor's done a great deal of work for charity, including supporting arts education, children's literacy and natural disaster relief, in recognition of which, in

2012, she was presented with a Kids' Choice Award by Michelle Obama, who praised her as someone who 'has rocketed to the top of the music industry but still keeps her feet on the ground, someone who has shattered every expectation of what a twenty-two-year-old can accomplish'. It was, if anything, an understatement.

Taylor attempts to remain fairly apolitical, saying, 'I don't think it's my job to try and influence people which way they should vote,' but it was pretty obvious where her sympathies lay when, following Barack Obama's election victory, she told *Rolling Stone* magazine, 'I've never seen this country so happy about a political decision in my entire time of being alive. I'm so glad this was my first election.' After which she went on to praise Michelle Obama as a role model.

As well as success, Taylor could match Harry in the romantic stakes, too. Her first high-profile boyfriend was the singer Joe Jonas, followed by the actor Taylor Lautner, famous for the *Twilight* films. There followed romances with the musician John Mayer, the actor Jake Gyllenhaal and Conor Kennedy, a scion of America's most famous political family. And then, in October 2012, she got together with Harry. It was a match made in show-business heaven: it upped both their profiles (not that either needed it), while at the same time, each understood the pressure the other was under. Simon Cowell himself couldn't have chosen a more suitable match for his protégé.

The relationship had been on the cards for some time. There had been rumours that Taylor fancied Harry from the first moment they met, and the feeling was clearly more than reciprocated. In the summer of 2012, some months before they finally got together, Harry couldn't hold back when talking to *Seventeen* magazine about Taylor: '[Taylor]'s a really lovely girl. Honestly, she couldn't be a sweeter person,' he said. 'She's a great girl and she's extremely talented. She's one of those people you meet [who's] genuinely a nice person. Some people you meet and they are not as nice as you make them out to be, but she's one of those people who's really just amazing.' And that was before they got together. Small wonder that Harry would go on to say he was in love.

Initially, no one who wasn't in the know suspected. Harry gave an interview to *OK!* magazine, in which he revealed that he had once jumped into bed with a friend's mother, but didn't let on that there was anyone special in his life at that moment: 'It was for a dare,' he said. 'She was asleep and she woke up when I got in, so I just ran down the stairs. She had a robe on, but I don't know if there was anything on underneath. I don't necessarily just look at women who are older, I like girls my own age as well. My relationship with Caroline was well-documented and it made it out as if I only liked older women.' Well, at twenty-two, Taylor was only four years older than Harry, so their relationship seemed unlikely to raise the same comments.

Some people still had totally the wrong end of the stick and Harry was often connected with Cara Delevingne. 'Cara's management think that Harry is the wrong image for her,' a source close to the model told the *Sun*. 'They believe that being linked with Harry could damage her high-end jobs. They want her to stay out of the papers. But if anything, it's just made Harry more keen. Telling two young people "no" is just going to make them want to meet up even more.'

Maybe, but Harry's interest now lay in a very different direction and finally, in November 2012, the real story broke. Harry and Taylor were seen holding hands and flirting at the American *X Factor* studio in Los Angeles, where he was introduced to Taylor's mother, Andrea. 'Harry turned up at rehearsals to watch Taylor. She delayed it twenty minutes to wait for him,' a source told the *Sun*. 'He was sitting with her mum Andrea and she seemed won over too. After Taylor finished, he picked her up over his shoulder and carried her to her trailer. They were holding hands and flirting all day. They had matching chains on and queued up together to get their lunch from the catering truck. It was all really sweet.'

But that wasn't all. A friend of Taylor's revealed that they'd already had a mini-fling and were now giving it another go. 'She thought Harry was hot and got Justin [Bieber] to introduce them,' he said. 'She fell for him straight away. They secretly had a bit of a thing. They were texting and talking a lot and met up a few times. But it ended when Harry was spotted with another girl in New Zealand. Taylor was really embarrassed by what happened and was nervous about giving him another go. But this time they have spent more time getting to know each other. Taylor is very full-on in relationships and falls for people quickly. Harry is being careful because he doesn't want to hurt her again. But he's made it clear he likes her a lot. They have been quietly seeing each other again for a little while now.'

Was Harry beginning to grow up? Those around him had spoken on a number of occasions about the fact that he wanted to have a proper relationship, and as well as being very talented, Taylor was also extremely pretty. Men found her just as attractive as women found Harry, and the two of them had clearly established quite a bond. Even Simon Cowell was happy to speak out about it: 'I wasn't at rehearsal, but heard about it when I came down,' he said. 'I think they are good together.' He was right.

It wasn't long before other eye-witnesses came forward, too. One was Mario Lopez, the host of the US *X Factor*. 'Taylor Swift was the guest and during rehearsals Harry came up and slapped me on the back and said, "Hey, Mario, how ya doing?" And I said, "What are you doing here?" And he sort of pointed towards Taylor. They walked away hand in hand.'

It was all very adorable, although quite a few people couldn't resist joking that, at twenty-two, Taylor was far too young for Harry – jokes the couple chose to ignore. Less amusing was the behaviour of the internet trolls who took to Twitter, posting the usual nonsense, including death threats. Taylor was a show-business veteran by now, though, and she had not only developed a thick skin, but knew all about the downsides of living in the public eye. Harry was also used to the fact that his girlfriends got a hard time. This relationship was different, though: it was serious and the pair were in love.

Taylor was very different from Harry's previous girlfriends in all sorts of ways. She had become famous partly because her songs were so autobiographical and other teenage girls were able to relate to them. Harry would have been aware of the fact that she wasn't slow to criticize those she felt had treated her badly: after Joe Jonas broke up with her over the phone, she posted a video on Myspace of a *Camp Rock* doll – a toy based on the character he played in a 2008 Disney movie – and said, 'See, this one even comes with a phone, so he can break up with other dolls.' If that wasn't enough, she wrote a song 'Forever and Always' about Joe, containing the line, 'You looked me in the eye and told me you loved me/ Were you just kidding?'

Another, 'Dear John', about her relationship with John Meyer, questioned why he'd treated someone so much younger than him that badly. 'That song really hit home with a lot of girls who had been through toxic relationships and had found their way to the other side of it,' she said. And just in case someone had missed the point, in another interview she added, 'I always write songs about my life. And if you're horrible to me I'm going to write a song about you and you are not going to like it. That's how I operate.' The message was clear: don't mess with Taylor.

Indeed, with some people calling her a maneater, it appeared that Harry really had met his match. Taylor Lautner may or may not have been the inspiration behind 'Back To December' ('I'd go back in time and change it, but I can't'), while Jake Gyllenhaal might have been the inspiration behind

'The Last Time', which Taylor said was about someone she couldn't rely on. 'You never know when he's going to leave, you never know when he's going to come back, but he always does come back.' Did any of this put Harry off? Absolutely not. Taylor was young, gorgeous and a challenge, and Harry was already in deep.

Taylor, on the other hand, had another problem: she was an extremely high-profile, rich and successful woman, and she needed a man who could cope with that. Some men are intimidated by going out with someone with Taylor's achievements and she knew that. 'I like a man to take control,' she said. 'It needs to be equal. If I feel too much like I'm wearing the pants, I start to feel uncomfortable and we break up.'

In Harry, she had found someone who was just as famous and successful as her, and if his bank account didn't yet match hers, it was certainly heading in the right direction. In many ways, the two of them couldn't have been better for one another, and they realized it, too. Taylor had previously spelled out a few no-nos for any potential boyfriend to American *Vogue*, and Harry hadn't ticked any of the boxes: 'If you need to put me down a lot in order to level the playing field or something? If you are threatened by some part of what I do and want to cut me down to size in order to make it even? That won't work either.' And then, 'Also, I can't deal with someone who's obsessed with privacy. People kind of care if there are two famous people dating. But no one cares that much. If you care about privacy to the point where we need to dig a tunnel under this restaurant so that we can leave? I can't do that.' Far from wanting privacy, Harry was delighted to be as public as possible. After an initial period of coyness, he might as well have carried a banner saying that he and Taylor were an item.

From then on, the couple were pretty open about their relationship. They were spotted at each other's performances, strolling through New York hand in hand and stopping to watch the sea lions in Central Park. The boys played a sell-out gig in Madison Square Garden – proof, if any were needed, of just how far they'd come – and celebrated afterwards in the Hudson Hotel, where Harry introduced Taylor to his mother, Anne. He then serenaded Taylor at the bash before the two of them duetted to 'Don't Go Breaking My Heart', the song made famous by Elton John and Kiki Dee, before Harry tweeted that it had been the best night of his life. Who could blame him? The evening had combined huge professional success with a public outing with his new love. Goodwill overflowed, with some people branding them 'Haylor'.

Goodwill from most quarters, that is. Harry's reputation as a ladies' man had gone before him, and locals from Taylor's home town were warning him to treat her well. 'My advice is for Harry to treat her nice,' said local councillor Scott Sprouse. 'Taylor means a heck of a lot to this town and, of course, everyone is very protective of her. She is a big star, a local girl and a role model to so many in Hendersonville. No one wants to see her hurt.'

Joni Worsham, head teacher at Hendersonville High School, agreed. 'Taylor has a special place in the heart of the people in Hendersonville,' she said. 'She is very well respected and loved, and people only want the best for her. They would not want to see her hurt in any way by a relationship that went wrong.' The message was clear: mess with Taylor and Harry would have the good people of Hendersonville on his back.

Not that he had any intention of treating her badly, because this time, Harry said, he was in love. At eighteen, Harry was at the age when most first big relationships happen, and in this he was no different from any ordinary Joe. It was just that in his case, it was going to be played out in the full public glare. The next step was a visit to the UK, where Harry treated Taylor to a pub meal at the Rising Sun in Derbyshire's Peak District, and were it not for the fact that they were internationally famous and globally feted, it could have been any young couple out on a date. Taylor was pictured with a handbag Harry had bought for her twenty-third birthday, and nor was the handbag her only present – Harry had also bought her earrings, perfume and, in reference to her age, twenty-three cupcakes.

Although both had their own professional commitments, when they were in the same country at the same time, they were inseparable. Taylor accompanied Harry when he went to get yet another tattoo, and after a brief, work-related separation, they assembled at the Canyons Resort in Utah for some pre-Christmas skiing – Harry was subsequently pictured with a bandaged chin, apparently the result of a skiing accident. In another clear sign of how serious the relationship was, Taylor's brother Austin accompanied them.

Shortly afterwards, Taylor was off again, this time to Australia, while Harry returned to Britain to spend Christmas with his family. He was pictured at a local bowling alley, cheerily posing with some fans, but absence certainly seemed to make the heart grow fonder, as by all accounts the two of them spent the Christmas period Skyping up to five times a day. Harry's present to her was an antique emerald bracelet: no relationship had been like this for him before.

They weren't apart for long, though. After Christmas, Harry flew to the States so they could spend New Year's Eve together (forgetting his passport en route, and having to have it couriered from Cheshire to Heathrow). Taylor was ringing in the New Year in New York's Times Square, and Harry was there to cheer her on. She was doing well professionally, too: her current album had been at the top of the US charts for seven weeks in a row. In a pair of tight leather trousers, Taylor looked every inch the desirable pop star, and after the gig they shared a very public kiss, a clear sign that they wanted everyone to know how happy they were. 'Get a room!' shrieked the media, and they did, as soon afterwards Harry whisked her straight back to his hotel. According to friends, Harry was now publicly declaring his love, and no one watching them could have been in any doubt that he was besotted.

After the new year celebrations, it was off to the British Virgin Islands for a break: the couple were staying on Virgin Gorda, where they were pictured good-naturedly mingling with fans, as well as spending plenty of time on their own.

However, the relationship was proving to be tempestuous. After a massive row, the pair split up, with Taylor flying home alone, and spokespeople for the couple confirming the relationship was over. Taylor was pictured looking pretty glum, while Harry consoled himself by going off to spend a day at Sir Richard Branson's Necker Island, where he did 'plenty of partying', according to a friend who was there. But that was not the end of it. In Taylor, Harry had found an equal. He had also had his first proper, adult relationship. The pair were not quite ready to let each other go.

14

Take Me Home

The stakes were high, and not just for One Direction. With the extraordinary success of their first album, the fact that they had broken the United States and the perception that they were in it for the longer term, an awful lot of people were benefiting from what was happening to the boys. Prime amongst them, of course, was Simon Cowell, the mastermind behind it all, but also songwriters, producers, video directors, stylists, outfitters, take-away pizza men and untold others were benefiting from the boys' success, so it was absolutely essential that they got the second album right.

It was important that they didn't present themselves as yet another here today/gone tomorrow boy band, and that they managed to stand out from the crowd. 'People think that a boy band is air-grabs and [being] dressed in all one colour,' Niall told the Canadian newspaper *National Post*. 'We're boys in a band. We're trying to do something different from what people would think is the typical kind of boy band. We're trying to do different kinds of music and we're just trying to be ourselves, not squeaky clean.' That applied to the new album as much as anything – they needed to do something that would set them apart.

The boys themselves were allowed to make some of the decisions about what went onto the album: given that they were the key to what had happened over the previous year, they needed to get their personalities on the record. Equally, though, the material had to be spot on commercially. Cowell let it be known that some of the best songwriting teams in the world were to submit potential tracks, but that every one had to be number-one material. If One Direction did as well with *Take Me Home* as they had with *Up All Night*, they really would be established as the most successful band in the world. In the end, they stuck with some of the people who had made their earlier offerings so successful, including the Swedes Carl Falk and Rami Yacoub, and the American Savan Kotecha. As unlikely as it seems, Sweden really is where it's at, as Falk himself has pointed out: 'Swedes have been making great pop songs since Abba,' he told the *Independent*. 'We love melodies and nice chord changes. That fits the market right now. Melody is back, pop is back and young girls want their pop idols again.'

The fact that the boys were allowed an input was made clear by Harry when talking to the *Sun*. 'We're always writing on the road and in hotels and airports,' he said. 'We don't ever want our music to sound like a forty-year-old man in an office has written it and given it to us to perform.' In fact, a lot of very good pop songs have been written by forty-year-old men in offices, but they were making the point that they wanted to speak, or rather sing, directly to their fans.

Niall also emphasized how much influence the band members had on the material. 'The way it works for us – I don't know how everyone else works but – people don't see the meetings that we do, the all-day meetings about the album, and the way the songs are going to be even listed on the back of the album and album artwork,' he told *MTV News*. 'We want to have the most control that we possibly can of everything that we do. Like at the moment, I'm just proofreading the single artwork for the next single. They don't see that.'

It's not much of an exaggeration to say that half the big names in the entertainment industry seemed to be involved in the writing and production of One Direction's new album, including Dr Luke, Ed Sheeran, McFly frontman Tom Fletcher, Shellback, Toby Gad and others too numerous to mention, all well-known veterans of the pop scene. Now there was the issue of what to call the album, and Niall explained that, too. 'We thought about it for a while,' he said on Ryan Seacrest's KIIS-FM show, 'because we all do a lot of travelling around the world and we get to see a lot of cool places, but the main thing is there's no place like home. It's always kind of nice to go home.' The title had another resonance, of course: there is nothing the fans would have liked better than to take the lot of them home, although Niall didn't go into that.

And so recording began in May 2012 in Stockholm. It was serious business, but Harry managed to make it sound like a bundle of larks, with the boys ordering take-outs while they laid down their tracks. 'We ate loads of fast food while recording,' he told the *Daily Mirror*. 'I think we were in one studio for about two weeks and it was just a rotation of a certain Thai restaurant and Portuguese chicken restaurant over and over again. It's very easy to get stuck in there – you end up with a studio tan, where you just go green because you've been inside for a week.' They then moved to the United States to finish recording and start the promotional trail.

The album tracks were: 'Live While We're Young'; 'Kiss You'; 'Little Things'; 'C'mon, C'mon'; 'Last First Kiss'; 'Heart Attack'; 'Rock Me'; 'Change My Mind'; 'I Would'; 'Over Again'; 'Back For You'; 'They Don't Know About Us' and 'Summer Love'.

The boys got songwriting credits on some of the tracks, which was important, as it meant they would receive songwriting royalties that would significantly increase the amount they earned from the album sales. It was also a clever move on behalf of their management. One of the reasons Take That imploded the first time around was that Gary Barlow received songwriting royalties and the others didn't, which meant that he earned far more than the rest of the band. Inevitably, it was the cause of a lot of bad feeling, and ensuring that nothing similar happened to One Direction was an attempt to safeguard the boys' long-term future, as well as giving them the credit they deserved, of course.

'Live While We're Young' was the well-received first single, and the boys were everywhere, with innumerable television appearances, including *The X Factor* on both sides of the Atlantic as well as in Italy, Australia and Sweden, *The Ellen DeGeneres Show*, *The Today Show*, the BBC's *Children in Need*, the Royal Variety Performance and concerts in numerous other venues, including the hugely successful one at New York's Madison Square Garden.

Even the boys seemed taken aback by the scale of that particular concert. There were 20,000 fans screaming for them, and Niall told them, 'This is the best night of our lives. You guys have travelled from all around the world and we cannot believe what has happened here tonight. Thank you so much.' Indeed, the streets were crammed with fans, many of whom hadn't just travelled huge distances, but were camping out on the streets overnight to make sure they didn't miss a thing. The scenes would have been overwhelming for music-business veterans, let alone for relative newcomers with only their second release.

Zayn felt the same as Niall, saying, 'I'm overwhelmed. I'm from a small town in Bradford. Things like this don't happen to people like me. I owe it all to you.' But things like this were happening to all of them, and they were having to get used to it. First-class travel, five-star hotels, screaming fans and the best of everything – this was now becoming their everyday life.

The show felt 'almost like the biggest showcase you've ever been to,' Rob Stringer, the head of Columbia Records, said the next day, and the stage was built to house a long runway, which meant the boys could high-five the audience and

serenade individuals. It was also the precursor to a fan con-
vention in New Jersey, which fans from more than thirty-five
countries from around the world would attend.

Take Me Home was released in November 2012 to spectacular critical success. In the UK it sold 94,000 copies in the
first two days, 155,000 in the first week and went to number
one. In the United States, it was the third highest weekly debut
album of 2012 (Taylor's *Red* was first), selling 540,000 copies
and going to number one. 'You get moments all the time that
kind of make you pinch yourself, some of them make you
quite emotional,' Harry told the *Daily Mirror*, talking about
the album's number one slot. 'Winning a BRIT was a big
moment because we were just so excited to be at the awards
in the first place. Selling out Madison Square Garden was
pretty amazing, too. Then we woke to the news that our UK
tour was sold out. It was crazy.'

The record got to the top of the charts in more than
thirty-five countries, selling over one million copies worldwide and breaking too many records to list here, although it
should be mentioned that they were the first boy band in US
chart history to get two number one albums in one calendar
year. They also released the next single from the album, 'Little
Things', of which more below, which also went to number
one, making One Direction the youngest act in the British
charts to have both a number one album and single at the
same time.

Take Me Home wasn't just a commercial success, though, it
was a critical one, too. Al Fox of *BBC Music* said it was

'Polished and dependable; despite its safety there are some show-stopping pop anthems present.' Matt Collar from *All-Music* wrote of an 'immediately catchy mix of dancey pop', which conveys 'the group's shared lead-vocal approach and peppy, upbeat image.' The *Boston Globe* editor Sarah Rodman said the album was 'uniformly sleek and upbeat', and 'as boy bands go, fans – and their wary parents – could do much worse.' Jon Caramanica of *The New York Times* commented that the album is 'far more mechanical' than their debut album *Up All Night*, and singled out Zayn for praise.

'Little Things', written by Ed Sheeran and Fiona Bevan about the flaws that make each person unique, was the second single and another number one. It was actually written when Ed was seventeen, but it got lost and only resurfaced again in time for One Direction to record it. 'The great thing about it is I wrote that song with a girl called Fiona Bevan when I was seventeen and we lost the song,' Ed told Capital FM in October 2012. 'I've kept in touch with Fiona, we've done gigs and stuff and about two months ago she sent me the tune and was like, "Oh, do you remember this?" I was like, "Yeah, I do remember that," and I was in the studio with the One Direction boys at the time and I was playing it and they were like, "We really like that." It's got one of my favourite lines that I've ever written in a song.'

The artwork had the boys dressed in their usual preppy style, with Harry wearing a bow tie, and while the reviews were a little mixed, with some commentators concerned that it might make girls fixate on their own insecurities, plenty of critics were won over. It was a 'sweet song', according to Amy Sciarretto of *PopCrush*, and 'lets their individual vocal styles shine, and they can sidestep that nonsense about being puppets who sing studio-created and overly treated songs'. Alexis Petridis in the *Guardian* liked it, too, saying it was 'noticeably more sophisticated lyrically and emotionally than anything else on the album'. It was 'touching', he said. The accompanying music video, which was directed by Vaughan Arnell, was also a bit more sophisticated, having been shot in black and white.

The song did well and the boys put in their usual round of promotional appearances, including a turn at the Royal Variety Performance, where the host for the evening, David Walliams – who arrived on stage via a jet pack – dressed up as a besotted female fan. They were in good company, as fellow performers included Girls Aloud, Robbie Williams and Neil Young. They were starting to attract a lot of admiration from their showbiz peers these days, too: 'I went to watch Coldplay in Florida and saw Chris Martin before they went on,' Harry told the *Daily Mirror*. 'He sang "What Makes You Beautiful" before the chorus of "Yellow" kicked in. That was so strange because he's an inspiration for me. I think he's so good, he's sick . . . he's a really nice guy too. It was one of those moments where I kind of paused for a second, I didn't quite believe it. You never expect something like that to happen.' In reality, though, *everything* was happening: they performed the song for *The Today Show* and drew a 15,000-strong crowd to Rockefeller Plaza, where the video was filmed, complete with bright red London phone boxes in the background. They also announced plans for a 3D film to be released in August 2013, directed by Morgan Spurlock, prompting yet more comparisons with The Beatles, who made a fair few films in their time.

Back in the wider world, Union J were booted off *The X Factor* but, as they pointed out, it's not always the winners who end up doing best. 'Nine times out of ten it's actually better not to win. It's exciting times for Union J,' said band member Jaymi Hensley. 'We get the option to really work on our artistry. We get the time but not the pressure of being the winners, to really sit down and work out what style of music we want to do and make us a brand. We have got a lot of positives out of this and they outweigh the negatives.'

'We hope this is just the start of Union J's career, and hopefully we can go on and do what One Direction and JLS have done,' added his band mate Josh Cuthbert. Of course, every boy band in the world wanted just a fraction of One Direction's success.

Another band who'd had an association with One Direction was McFly. They'd been very pleased with the work they'd done on the new album, and voiced the hope that the relationship would continue. 'It's quite a selective process, writing for other bands,' said singer Tom Fletcher to the *Daily Star*. 'I don't want to write a song for just anyone. I only do it for people I really like because that's when you do your best work, so I hope the relationship we have with One Direction can continue. I love great pop music. When "What Makes

You Beautiful" came out it was like a breath of fresh air. It's perfect pop, and you don't think about anything else. The new Taylor Swift single is the same.'

For Taylor was having as much of an impact on the charts as on the gossip columns. Her relationship with Harry might have been up in the air, but both of them remain as professional as ever where their work was concerned.

One Direction appeared on the prestigious *10 Most Fascinating People of 2012* series, presented by the veteran talkshow host Barbara Walters, where they all confessed to having thoughts of getting married and settling down. In the meantime, a friend of Harry's from the old days, William Rogers, who used to play football with the young Harry back in Cheshire, gave an interview to the *Daily Star* in which he revealed that Harry's popularity with the girls was nothing new. 'I've known him since he was four years old,' he said. 'I know it sounds funny, but even in primary school he always had a few girls on the go. It was rather amusing. From Year Four, when he was about ten, Harry started with proper girlfriends. He's just had this unbelievable way with girls all his life, and it looks like none of that has changed. Harry was always the charmer with the little cheeky grin on his face. We played football together all the way up until high school. We're still mates. He's a great guy. He was always a really, really nice guy and got on well with everyone. He was very well liked, even then. I was never very successful with the girls but Harry's just got that special something. It's hard to explain.'

The fans understood it, though, and there were an awful lot of them. Comparisons were still being made with the Rolling Stones, and in particular between Harry and Mick Jagger, but the younger band were undeniably winning on the ticketing front. It emerged that One Direction had been the most popular live band of 2012. According to ticket website *Viagogo*, their tickets were selling at a record rate of two per second, outselling the Stones by three to one. And unlike the Stones, they were still recording, too.

The big one was still to come, though: the tour of 2013. The boys were now a big enough name to warrant their own private plane, which would not only make travelling more comfortable, but would relieve a good deal of the stress attached to going through airports.

In all, it had been an extraordinary year for Harry and his band mates in every possible sense. At the start of 2013, Harry found himself one of the most famous and successful singers in the world having enjoyed a relationship with one of the most famous and successful singers in the world. Opportunities were flooding in, the band was breaking records right, left and centre and they were absolutely adored everywhere. And what's more the year ahead looked set to be even better still.

15

The Only Direction is Up

So what was it that made One Direction and, above all, Harry, stand out? There have been an awful lot of boy bands through the years, some of whom have been successful and some not, but even the successful ones, such as the great Take That, hadn't achieved what the boys had managed. To succeed over and over and over again, especially in the United States, the toughest market of them all, took some doing. Why had One Direction succeeded where so many others had failed?

For a start, it was because what you saw was what you got. They may have been a manufactured band, but each was utterly true to himself. None of them had adopted personas, no one was keeping a dark side hidden, and given how open they were about their female friends, there was nothing to hide on that front either. The five of them complemented each other perfectly, and yet Harry still stood out. His good looks and easy charm would have stood him in good stead whatever walk of life he'd chosen, but as a pop star he was perfect. Fresh-faced and with all that hair, even among the good-looking members of One Direction he managed to stand out.

Another element that worked in their favour was talent. An awful lot of manufactured bands are put together on a looks-alone basis, but all of One Direction could genuinely sing. The critics often commented on this, too. 'The stripped down set both showed off Horan's ability to play guitar, as well as One Direction's admirable live vocals,' wrote Erica Futterman of *Rolling Stone*. 'There was no need to worry about a backing track or a bum note, a pleasant realization at a pop show.'

'It's easy to get lost in the inherent appeal of their perfectly coiffed dos and almost-too-put-together preppy style, but somewhere in the midst of all the love-struck squeals of teenage girls are guys who can actually sing and, to a certain extent, entertain,' said Melody Lau of the *National Post*. And Jane Stevenson of *Canoe* thought, 'What I didn't really prepare myself for was that they can all actually sing in concert ... And there's none of that choreographed dance move nonsense. Instead, One Direction, backed by a four-piece band, moved naturally through a pretty classy, low-key production that saw them in different settings thanks to three video screens – beach, school, party, winter cabin, and dinner party – in various preppy-inspired outfits. They all looked like they'd just climbed out of an Abercrombie & Fitch ad.'

That was certainly true and the image didn't hurt one jot. It could also be said that One Direction had filled a gaping hole in the market. There was Justin Bieber, of course, but there was just one Justin compared with five One Directioners, and a band always has a different appeal to a solo artist.

Not better, just different. Nor was there anyone else out there doing exactly what the boys were doing. The Wanted might be a boy band, but they appealed to a slightly different type of fan and didn't have the same innocence and boyishness.

Neil McCormick of the *Daily Telegraph* summed it up perfectly. 'It took the meteoric rise of Justin Bieber (a Canadian) to demonstrate that there was still a huge appetite for clean-cut, wholesome, whiter-than-white, middle-class parent-friendly pop: cute boys advocating puppy love,' he wrote. 'And what could be better than one cute boy, if not five? It is no coincidence that The Wanted share a manager with Bieber, and One Direction are the same age as him (and still several years younger than most of their rivals).'

Then there was the effect of social media, which was used in marketing the group as never before. As Sonny Takhar, chief executive of Syco Records, had already pointed out, social media had become the new radio, playing an all-important part in breaking their act globally. Will Bloomfield, the group's manager, agreed. 'These guys live online, and so do their fans,' he said. To prove the point, One Direction's Twitter account had attracted five million followers by July 2012, with the account gaining followers at an average of 20,000 per day.

'For the most part that just means the group presents themselves as typical, goofy and uncensored teenage boys – posting jokey YouTube videos, for instance, or boozing at awards shows,' wrote Leah Collins in the *National Post*.

Meanwhile, Kitty Empire said in the *Observer*, 'Dance routines are fundamental to the boy band – or at least, to 90s

Take That and late-oos JLS. One Direction fulfil a great many boy-band prerequisites (looks, soppy lyrics, tune-grasp, fame-lust) but their lack of routines points to the subtle digressions afoot here.'

So where next? The boys had already managed to do what so many before them had failed to do by cracking America, and with more tours and albums on the way, their popularity seemed certain to continue to grow. Of Harry himself, ultimately a solo career almost certainly awaits. Against stiff competition, he's stolen the limelight from his band mates, attracted attention effortlessly and has those twin attributes that money just can't buy – charisma and star quality – which should stand him in good stead.

Harry seems likely to remain firmly in the spotlight, with his talent for attracting controversy, deliberately or otherwise – sometimes in his choice of partner, sometimes just by what he says – none of which bodes ill for a long-lasting career.

The groups the boys have been most often compared with are the Rolling Stones and Take That. Harry has been directly compared to Mick Jagger, who has had one of the most successful careers in the history of rock music, while Take That are possibly the most loved entertainers in the land. If Harry, with or without his band mates, can follow these examples then he's in for a very long career. Mick Jagger ended up getting a knighthood. Sir Harry Styles? It's a thought – about fifty years from now . . .